CONTENTS

NEW DIRECTIONS FOR TEACHING AND LEARNING

Marilla D. Svinicki, *University of Texas, Austin*
EDITOR-IN-CHIEF

R. Eugene Rice, *American Association for Higher Education*
CONSULTING EDITOR

Fresh Approaches to the Evaluation of Teaching

Christopher Knapper
Queen's University, Kingston, Canada

Patricia Cranton
University of New Brunswick

EDITORS

Number 88, Winter 2001

 JOSSEY-BASS
A Wiley Company
www.josseybass.com

FRESH APPROACHES TO THE EVALUATION OF TEACHING
Christopher Knapper, Patricia Cranton (eds.)
New Directions for Teaching and Learning, no. 88
Marilla D. Svinicki, Editor-in-Chief
R. Eugene Rice, Associate Editor

Microfilm copies of issues and articles are available in 16mm and 35mm, as well as microfiche in 105mm, through University Microfilms Inc., 300 North Zeeb Road, Ann Arbor, Michigan 48106-1346.

ISSN 0271-0633   electronic ISSN 1536-0768   ISBN 0-7879-5790-9

NEW DIRECTIONS FOR TEACHING AND LEARNING is part of The Jossey-Bass Higher and Adult Education Series and is published quarterly by Jossey-Bass, 989 Market Street, San Francisco, California 94103-1741 Periodicals postage paid at San Francisco, California, and at additional mailing offices. Postmaster: Send address changes to New Directions for Teaching and Learning, Jossey-Bass, 989 Market Street, San Francisco, California 94103-1741

New Directions for Teaching and Learning is indexed in College Student Personnel Abstracts, Contents Pages in Education, and Current Index to Journals in Education (ERIC).

SUBSCRIPTIONS cost $65 for individuals and $130 for institutions, agencies, and libraries. Prices subject to change.

EDITORIAL CORRESPONDENCE should be sent to the editor-in-chief, Marilla D. Svinicki, The Center for Teaching Effectiveness, University of Texas at Austin, Main Building 2200, Austin, TX 78712-1111.

Cover photograph by Richard Blair/Color & Light © 1990.

www.josseybass com

FROM THE SERIES EDITORS

About This Publication. Since 1980, *New Directions for Teaching and Learning* has brought a unique blend of theory, research, and practice to leaders in postsecondary education. We strive not only for substance but also for timeliness, compactness, and accessibility.

The series has four goals: to inform readers about current and future directions in teaching and learning in postsecondary education, to illuminate the context that shapes these new directions, to illustrate these new directions through examples from real settings, and to propose ways in which the new directions can be incorporated into still other settings.

This publication reflects the view that teaching deserves respect as a high form of scholarship. We believe that significant scholarship is done not only by the researcher who reports results of empirical investigations but also by practitioners who share with others disciplined reflections about teaching. Contributors to NDTL approach questions of teaching and learning as seriously as they approach substantive questions in their own disciplines, and they deal not only with pedagogical issues but with the intellectual and social context out of which those issues arise. Authors deal on the one hand with theory and research and on the other with practice, and they translate from research and theory to practice and back again.

About This Volume. An ongoing struggle in higher education is finding ways of evaluating teaching that reflect its complex nature. Institutions are looking for new alternatives beyond student evaluations and finding some in the new perspectives and technologies that have been emerging in recent years. This issue of *New Directions for Teaching and Learning* gives faculty and administrators alike some good ideas about alternative sources and formats for evaluating teaching.

MARILLA D. SVINICKI, *Editor-in-Chief*

R. EUGENE RICE, *Associate Editor*

EDITORS' NOTES

The evaluation of teaching is one of those vexed issues that is much debated but never quite resolved. There are probably more books and papers on instructional evaluation than on any other topic in the higher education literature. However, a good deal of what is written is narrowly focused and endlessly covers old ground. In particular, the merits and shortcomings of student ratings of teaching have been exhaustively discussed. Despite major criticisms, student questionnaires continue to be the dominant method for evaluating teaching across North America, and the approaches used today are, in fact, remarkably similar to those of two decades ago.

This volume takes a new tack by exploring alternative approaches to assessing teaching performance. Although student ratings are mentioned in passing, they are not the main focus here. Rather, the goal is to explore a wide range of methods for documenting and judging teaching that have often been overlooked in the sometimes acrimonious debates about the reliability and validity of student questionnaires.

Chapter One sets the scene by raising some underlying issues and principles that affect all forms of evaluation—determining criteria, making links between teaching methods and learning outcomes, and distinguishing between evaluation for self-improvement and evaluation for accountability. In Chapter Two, Patricia Cranton argues that knowledge about teaching can be communicative and emancipatory as well as instrumental, and she describes a concept of evaluation that is primarily interpretive and critical in nature, offering a range of relevant strategies.

One of the most widely used alternatives to sole reliance on student ratings is the teaching portfolio; in Chapter Three, two of the Canadian pioneers of this approach describe its history, goals, and applications. Next, Ellen Carusetta reminds us that we have been documenting and evaluating teaching for many years for the purpose of making teaching awards; in Chapter Four, she outlines the strengths and weaknesses of the adjudication process.

Chapter Five examines the role of technology in teaching evaluation and makes a plea for recognizing the principles of good evaluation practice as evaluation systems are increasingly being automated.

Since Ernest Boyer first coined the term *scholarship of teaching* over a decade ago, it has captured the imagination of many academics who wish to see college teaching achieve a higher profile. Chapter Six explores the distinction among good teaching, scholarly teaching, and teaching scholarship and explores the role of formative evaluation in relation to these concepts.

The last three chapters explore more systemic and institutional aspects of evaluation. Chapter Seven focuses on the tricky issue of evaluating teaching effectiveness in terms of student learning outcomes. Chapter Eight describes the role of evaluation in the accreditation of university teachers. And Chapter Nine examines the evaluation of teaching for entire programs, departments, and institutions.

The contributions to this volume remind us that not only are there many different ways and sources of evidence for teaching evaluation but that the goals and criteria for evaluation can also vary. Because evaluation is inevitable, the main challenge is to ensure that we use the best methods for the right purposes. The chapters in this volume should help us make those choices.

Christopher Knapper
Patricia Cranton
Editors

1

It is not a question of whether teaching should be evaluated but a matter of how. Recent years have seen promising trends away from a simple reliance on student ratings toward more broadly based and comprehensive approaches.

Broadening Our Approach to Teaching Evaluation

Christopher Knapper

Although evaluative judgments are part of everyday living, knowing we are about to be evaluated tends to send a shiver down our spine. In our hearts we know that evaluation can be good for us; it can provide useful insights that help us do things differently and better. Yet most of us hate to be evaluated, whether it is in our personal, social, or working lives. And this is especially true when important decisions hinge on the results of the evaluation, such as when we take a final examination or a driving test. This is certainly the case with the evaluation of teaching—an activity where a good deal of self-esteem is involved.

Just as the assessment of students is perhaps the task that faculty like least, the evaluation of teaching performance can be fraught with unpleasantness—even controversy. Student ratings of university teachers have been common for at least thirty years, but it is a rare campus where they are accepted with equanimity. It is now also increasingly common to review teaching quality in entire departments and programs (see Wergin and Swingen, 2000), but these assessments are often resisted as simply invalid and inaccurate time wasters. Yet evaluation—of teaching and of our other professional and personal activities—is inevitable. We go through each day making thousands of evaluations (about the weather, last night's movie, our partner's new haircut, a political decision we read about in the paper, the quality of our midmorning coffee). We are even content to quantify our evaluations; we enjoy the star system for restaurants and movies and the points awarded to products in *Consumer Reports*.

In the last analysis, as Cranton points out (see Chapter Two), most evaluative judgments are subjective, even though we may make use of quantitative data to help with our decisions. What's important to recognize

NEW DIRECTIONS FOR TEACHING AND LEARNING, no 88, Winter 2001 © John Wiley & Sons, Inc

3

is that such judgments will be made even in the absence of good data. Just as many of us feel we know that University X is good and University Y is outstanding, students and colleagues quickly form impressions of a professor's teaching abilities, as well as the quality of instruction in different academic departments. Evaluation will take place, even in the absence of solid evidence, based on such sources as hearsay and gossip. And teaching is such an important activity for universities that we would be well advised to make the process as informed and helpful as possible. How can this best be done?

Criteria for Evaluation

One good starting point is to decide on our goals and criteria for the evaluation of teaching, which in turn means having some consensus on what we understand "good teaching" to be. Yet it is surprising that either this is often not done or such criteria are implicit and never openly discussed. Even in the case of prestigious teaching awards offered by national bodies and individual institutions (see Chapter Four), the basis for judgment may be obscure, which can lead to controversy and scepticism.

When we put a general statement on an evaluation form such as, "On the whole, how good was this teacher?" we are, in effect, asking students to use their *own* definition and criteria for good teaching on the assumption that worth is in the eye of the beholder. And by including questions about organization, fair grading, quality of feedback, enthusiasm, and concern for students' needs, we are *imposing* criteria, even if we might not recognize the fact.

Whose criteria should count the most: those of the students (the recipients of teaching), the faculty (who presumably have more expertise in pedagogy), some external agency such as the government, some professional association, or an employer? Or, to tackle the question in a different way, is there a body of evidence to which we might turn to show that certain characteristics of teaching are related to particular learning outcomes? If so, this evidence would be helpful in guiding the choice of dimensions and processes for evaluation.

Even here, though, complications arise, to which Fenwick has alluded in Chapter Seven, having to do with the general purposes of education. For example, if we believe that the goal of higher education is to train students for jobs, that belief dictates one set of outcomes. (In this case the outcomes of job placement or lifetime salary are relatively easy to measure and are frequently used by higher education institutions to justify the excellence of their teaching programs.) However, the belief that higher education exists primarily to prepare students for citizenship or help them develop as lifelong learners would suggest another set of outcomes.

Links Between Teaching Methods and Learning Outcomes.   Despite these caveats, having information about the relationship between teaching processes and their effects on learning would certainly be useful in helping design evaluation schemes. In the case of lectures, for example, there is some evidence that exam performance is helped by such factors as teacher clarity, organization, enthusiasm, and rapport with students (see Centra, 1993, and d'Apollonia and Abrami, 1997, for a review of the relevant research). In practice, performance on exams in a single course is of less importance over the long term than the impact of an entire program of study on students' values, attitudes, and the learning habits they will take with them into other aspects of their lives. This is clearly a much trickier issue, but there is emerging evidence about the effects of teaching programs and academic climate on student learning approaches.

For example, the extensive research by Astin (1993) and Pascarella and Terenzini (1991) has examined aspects of teaching that influence cognitive development in students. (Their findings are rather surprising for the large number of factors that apparently have no effect at all, which might indicate that students themselves have more to do with successful learning than the influence of particular teachers or courses.) The classic study by Ramsden and Entwistle (1981) identifies a number of factors that encourage deep learning approaches in students, including workload, use of active learning methods, type of assessment tasks that are set, interpersonal contact between teacher and students, and so on. The Course Experience Questionnaire (CEQ), now used routinely in Australian universities to evaluate teaching effectiveness at the departmental and institutional level (described briefly in Chapter Nine), is an approach to evaluation built on this research. Along similar lines, Kember has shown links between university teachers' approach to teaching and changes in the learning approaches of their students. In particular, teachers who adopt more learner-centered methods (more active learning tasks and less reliance on didactic lectures) tend to foster deeper learning (Kember, 1997; Kember and Gow, 1994).

Although the linking of evaluation methods to specific and agreed-upon educational and learning goals is time consuming and difficult, it is certainly worth the effort, not just because it produces better evaluation but because the whole process helps stimulate debate about the university's central mission: teaching and learning. As described by Fenwick, Alverno College is one institution that has embedded ongoing evaluation into its programs. Moreover, it has done so in a consultative manner, involving both faculty and students in the process. Here evaluation is seen as an essential component of learning, not simply something tacked on at the end of a course for largely bureaucratic reasons. Alverno's linking of institutional goals to both the assessment of students and the evaluation of learning outcomes is an example of Biggs's notion of *alignment* (see Chapter Nine).

Summative and Formative Evaluation. One other aspect of the goals of evaluation concerns the *formative* versus *summative* distinction (terms originally used by Michael Scriven, whom Cannon quotes at the beginning of Chapter Nine). As more and more faculty in North American universities have become unionized, the evaluation of individual performance has

been increasingly seen as part of the terms of employment and thus nego-
tiable as part of a collective bargaining agreement. This in turn has tended
to sharpen the distinction between evaluation for accountability purposes
and evaluation that is intended primarily to give feedback that can serve as
a basis for reflection about teaching and possible changes or improvements.
(Approaches to formative evaluation are described in Chapter Six.)

Although it has become a cliché that evaluation methods well suited
for one purpose are often much less appropriate for another, there is considerable overlap between these two types of evaluation. Wright and
Knapper make the point in Chapter Three that teaching portfolios prepared
for one purpose (say, annual review) almost inevitably serve another (self-
reflection about teaching). Similarly, undertaking a departmental review,
although it may be intended primarily for administrative or accountability
purposes, will stimulate reflection and debate about goals and priorities in
all but the most moribund and cynical academic unit. At the same time,
there is no question that before institutions, units, or individuals undertake
an evaluation of teaching, they should carefully consider the motives for
evaluating, the purpose the information will serve, and what actions might
be taken as a result to undertake possible future change. If these questions
have not been considered (and satisfactorily answered), it is doubtful that
the evaluation will achieve anything of value.

The Changing Context for Evaluation

University teaching has been largely unscrutinized, perhaps because it is
done in private—or, at least, out of the sight of colleagues and administrators. In medieval universities, students voted with their feet, either by
stamping them to show disapproval or by simply abandoning the class alto-
gether. In more recent times, evaluation has relied primarily on student
questionnaires. This has always been problematic in the sense that effective
learning (presumably the main goal of teaching) is dependent on far more
than an individual instructor or course. For example, learning also depends
on the motivation, prior knowledge, values, and attitudes of students, as
well as the amount of independent work they undertake. This, in turn, is
affected by demographic, social, and institutional factors, in particular the
academic climate in the university and home department. Yet teaching evaluation has traditionally focused on individuals, not organizations.

The Call for Accountability. Although there is a long history of
reviewing academic departments and entire institutions (for example, for
accreditation purposes, as Beaty describes in Chapter Eight), the attention
paid to teaching in these exercises has generally been superficial and has
relied mainly on describing curriculum content and the qualifications of faculty, perhaps supplemented by evidence of student performance on exams.
One recent change, as reflected by many of the chapters in this volume, is
the broadening of evaluation from a focus on individuals to a scrutiny of

larger units and the widening of the scope and methods used, often including both qualitative appraisals and quantitative data.

It is increasingly being recognized that evaluation methods used in the past are inappropriate at a time when many profound changes are affecting higher education. For example, we now have a much more diverse student population, and there is concern to provide equal opportunities for students of different backgrounds and abilities to learn and succeed in college. The last decade has seen a rapid growth of educational technology, distance education, and on-line learning. The role and influence of an individual instructor in these approaches may be much less clear than in a traditional lecture course. Technology has, in fact, changed the way evaluation itself takes place, as Theall and Franklin describe in Chapter Five. Other factors are political and financial. Students in many universities pay much higher fees than they did in the past and have started to regard themselves as "consumers" of an educational "product." This, in turn, is part of a move toward market-driven higher education in which the purpose of a university seems largely to fulfil strategic objectives, often dictated by business interests (see Levine, 2001). All these issues affect approaches to the evaluation of teaching; in particular, they reinforce the importance of accountability, both internal and external.

The Stakeholders in Evaluation. The questionnaire-based teacher ratings that date back to at least the 1960s were initiated by students, primarily as an aid to selecting courses and teachers (hence the criticism of student evaluations as a popularity contest). To this day, a number of student governments publish "anti-calendars" that summarize the results of student ratings. A powerful stimulus for the development of teaching portfolios (see Chapter Three) was the aim of having individual faculty members take control of the evaluation process by broadening the basis of teaching appraisal. Not only are faculty the focus of most teaching evaluation but they play a major role as evaluators, especially through service on tenure, promotion, and appointment committees.

Other potential stakeholders in the evaluation of teaching include university administrators, employers, parents, and the government. This has led to externally imposed evaluation systems such as the academic audits and collection of performance indicators of teaching, as discussed in Chapters Seven and Nine. (The issue of measuring education "quality" has such currency that there is a journal with the title, *Quality in Higher Education.*) And Beaty, in Chapter Eight, describes the steps taken in the United Kingdom to introduce accreditation for university teachers. This has led to interesting debates about teaching standards and criteria, appropriate training for new entrants to the profession, and methods of evaluating their effectiveness. It is interesting that the preferred method of documenting and appraising teaching is an expanded version of the teaching portfolio.

With multiple stakeholders, one challenge is to devise an approach to evaluation that can serve different (and possibly conflicting) needs. This is an almost impossible task and often produces acrimonious disagreements between representatives of the different constituencies. For example, information that is useful for one purpose (for example, a student selecting a college or a department head assigning teaching loads) may be unhelpful or even harmful for other purposes, such as providing feedback to a beginning teacher. Negotiating a balance of interests among stakeholders can be a delicate matter and requires extensive compromise.

In my own university a committee of faculty, students, and administrators devised a system of evaluation based on a combination of student ratings and teaching portfolios. Each agreed to sacrifice elements of evaluation that they would like to have kept. For example, department heads and students wanted to see the open-ended comments written on the rating forms, but this was thought to be undesirable from the point of the view of the individual teacher (especially in the case of beginning teachers). The latter would have preferred the ratings be confidential, but student government representatives naturally wished to have publicly available data for purposes of accountability. Although the committee reached a delicate consensus, and the system put in place worked reasonably well, the original process leading to this balance of interests was soon forgotten, and political pressures subsequently led to changes in the system that pleased no one.

Conclusions

A decade ago a monograph about university teaching evaluation would have been primarily concerned with the reliability and validity of student ratings. Student evaluations are certainly discussed in these pages, but the broad range of alternative approaches dealt with in later chapters indicates how much evaluation has changed. The contributions that follow not only reflect the interest of a much broader range of stakeholders but introduce alternative evaluation processes that are already changing practice. Some of these methods have been borrowed from other sources (for example, outcomes assessment, performance indicators, and academic audits); others, such as the teaching portfolio, have been devised specifically for academic purposes.

This broader and more eclectic approach to evaluation is, in my view, a good thing, as is the increased attention being paid to underlying goals and the interests of different stakeholders. Although this makes evaluation more complex, it forces us back to first principles and makes us examine not just the criteria and rationale for evaluation but the goals of higher education itself and the question of whose interests we serve. From the point of view of the individual faculty member, the new emphasis on outcomes and accountability may seem threatening. However, if university teaching is to be a professional activity (as Beaty describes), then the honest appraisal of ourselves and our peers is surely an inherent part of our role and obligations as a teacher. And it is an essential component of the scholarship of teaching (see Chapter Six), if we are to gather data that can improve our own practice and inform a more general understanding of effective teaching strategies. Furthermore, the proper evaluation of teaching and reflection about what it reveals can lead us to raise critical questions about teaching values and practices that are part of what Cranton, in Chapter Two, refers to as "emancipatory knowledge" and an openness to alternatives.

As stated at the outset of this chapter, it is not a matter of whether we evaluate teaching but rather a question of how we do it. What ends do we have in mind, and who controls the process? If academics fail to take responsibility for evaluation of teaching, it is clear that others will be eager to do so.

References

Astin, A. W. *What Matters in College? Four Critical Years Revisited.* San Francisco: Jossey-Bass, 1993.

Centra, J. A. *Reflective Faculty Evaluation: Enhancing Teaching and Determining Faculty Effectiveness.* San Francisco: Jossey-Bass, 1993.

d'Apollonia, S., and Abrami, P. C. "Navigating Student Ratings of Instruction." *American Psychologist,* 1997, 52, 1198–1208.

Kember, D. "A Reconceptualisation of the Research into University Academics' Conceptions of Teaching." *Learning and Instruction,* 1997, 7, 255–275.

Kember, D., and Gow, L. "Orientations to Teaching and their Effect on the Quality of Student Learning." *Journal of Higher Education,* 1994, 65, 58–74.

Levine, A. "The Remaking of the American University." *Innovative Higher Education,* 2001, 25, 253–267.

Pascarella, E. T., and Terenzini, P. T. *How College Affects Students.* San Francisco: Jossey-Bass, 1991.

Ramsden, P., and Entwistle, N. J. "Effects of Academic Departments on Students' Approaches to Studying." *British Journal of Educational Psychology,* 1981, 51, 368–383.

Wergin, J. F., and Swingen, J. N. *Departmental Assessment: How Some Campuses Are Effectively Evaluating the Collective Work of Faculty.* Washington, D.C.: American Association for Higher Education, 2000.

CHRISTOPHER KNAPPER *is director of the Instructional Development Centre at Queen's University in Kingston, Ontario.*

2

When we see knowledge about teaching as communicative and emancipatory in nature, we are led to view the evaluation of teaching as interpretive and critical processes.

Interpretive and Critical Evaluation

Patricia Cranton

We have become quite familiar with the notion that we should be matching the kinds of techniques we use for the evaluation of learning with the nature of the expected learning outcomes. We use multiple-choice tests to assess the recognition and recall of facts; we use essays to evaluate the more complex synthesis and integration of ideas. Even though not all faculty are skilled at matching the tests they use to their teaching goals, there is an underlying sense of striving for fairness and, at the same time, a recognition that the evaluation of student learning is often subjective. It calls on our subject area expertise, our knowledge, and interpretation. We make judgments based on our perception of what constitutes good thinking and good work in the discipline.

When it comes to evaluating teaching, we seem to have long been stuck in the rut of thinking that we need to attach numbers to our assessment in order to make it as objective as possible. Consequently, the use of student ratings has long dominated the evaluation of the teaching process. Of course, student ratings of instruction are in fact subjective perceptions based on students' knowledge about good teaching. But we remain reassured by the charts, frequencies, means, and standard deviations produced by this assessment technique. We have the illusion of objectivity.

In this chapter, I suggest we rethink and critically examine some of our taken-for-granted assumptions about the evaluation of teaching. I propose a perspective that takes into account the nature of knowledge about teaching. First, I outline three kinds of knowledge, as described by Habermas (1971). I then argue that knowledge about teaching is primarily communicative and emancipatory in nature. This leads me to the interpretive and critical paradigms as ways of thinking about evaluating teaching. Finally, I suggest practical strategies for the evaluation of teaching—strategies congruent with the interpretive and critical paradigms.

Three Domains of Knowledge

Habermas (1971) describes three basic human interests, each of which leads us to acquire a different kind of knowledge. Our technical interests lead us to *instrumental knowledge*. Technical interests come from the need to control and manipulate our environment so as to obtain shelter, food, transportation, and, of course, technological advances. A quick glance around our home or office reveals the incredible products of our technical interests—the buildings in which we live and work, the car or train we use to travel from one to the other, the refrigerator and microwave oven, the computer and fax machine, the Internet and e-mail. Instrumental knowledge is based on invariant cause-and-effect principles. Through instrumental knowledge, we can predict events in the world. A stone thrown into the air will always fall back to earth, regardless of which culture or community we are in when we throw the stone. The laws of gravity are invariant. Instrumental knowledge is objective and empirically derived, thus falling into the philosophical realm of positivism.

Our practical interests lead to what Habermas (1971) calls *practical knowledge* and what others (Mezirow, 1997, for example) call *communicative knowledge*. I choose to use the term *communicative knowledge* here, as it is more descriptive of this domain. We have an interest in living together in a society and coordinating social actions so as to satisfy individual and social needs. We have to live and work together. We therefore need to understand each other, both on a simple personal level and on a larger social and political level. This understanding constitutes communicative knowledge, which is acquired through language. It is a knowledge of the norms underlying the society we live in, whether these involve interpersonal relationships, groups, communities, organizations, cultures, nations, or the global society. Validity is determined by consensus within a group and a sense of rightness or morality. What is agreed-upon knowledge in one culture may not be valid in another culture. Our justice systems, social systems, and political systems are based on communicative knowledge. The philosophical foundation for communicative knowledge lies in hermeneutics.

Our emancipatory interests lead to *emancipatory knowledge*. We have an interest in growth, development, self-awareness, freedom from constraint or oppression, and relational autonomy. We are constrained by uncritically assimilated norms, beliefs, and values. We absorb the social norms and systems of our community and culture, and when these norms are unquestioned or become unquestionable, we are oppressed, even though we may not be aware of it, in the sense that we do not know about alternatives. Emancipatory knowledge is acquired through critical reflection and critical self-reflection. Our basic human drive for growth can lead us to critically question assumptions, values, beliefs, norms, and perspectives. Philosophically, the underpinnings of emancipatory knowledge lie in critical theory.

Knowledge About Teaching

Although it can be argued that knowledge about teaching that is empirically derived is instrumental, this may be a specious argument. Using the empirical-analytical research paradigm to derive knowledge does not, in itself, make that knowledge instrumental. It could well be that the use of empirical methodologies is inappropriate to begin with. Following the definition of instrumental knowledge as consisting of objective, invariant, cause-and-effect principles, we find very little instrumental knowledge about teaching. What works—what forms good teaching in higher education—is influenced by many factors, including discipline, level of instruction, class size, the characteristics of the students, and the characteristics and behavior of the teacher. In other words, what constitutes good teaching depends on the individuals who are working and learning together, as well as the social context within which the teaching takes place. We can find very few, if any, rules telling us that if we do this, learning will always take place. If we examine the commonly espoused principles of effective teaching, we find that they are not invariant. For instance, is it always better to be well organized in our teaching? Some students may feel stifled by structure. Some teachers may be naturally more intuitive and free flowing in their style. Some subject areas may not lend themselves to a clear organization. Perhaps students' critical thinking is enhanced by unexpected twists and turns in the class proceedings. Or is discussion always better than a lecture? If students are acquiring instrumental knowledge, reading or practicing will be more appropriate than discussion. Some students may not learn best from discussion. In some large classes, discussion may be inconvenient and time consuming, or even chaotic and distracting. What works best depends on the people and the context. There is no one way of teaching. We have some generalizations that are informed by empirical research, but we have no invariable truths. This means that in spite of our desire to have instrumental knowledge about teaching, there is very little of it. The understanding of interpersonal relationships, groups, and educational systems is communicative knowledge; this understanding informs teaching.

Communicative knowledge about teaching exists at different levels. At the broadest level, we understand the role of education in society, the responsibility of educators in social action and reform, the relationship between the university or college and the community it serves, and the goals of higher education. Within our department or discipline, we understand, for example, the goals of the program, how a program fits into the mission of the institution, how the various components of a curriculum are related to each other, and how research and teaching within the discipline are integrated. In the classroom, we develop a knowledge of group processes, our relationship with students, our own teaching style and preferences, how to give useful feedback, and how to best present or work with the various facets of the subject area. In our relationship with students, we understand, for instance, learning styles and other individual differences, motivation, students' developmental stages, how to foster independence or self-direction, and how students best learn different aspects of the course content.

The desire to grow and develop as teachers leads us to emancipatory knowledge about teaching. When we critically question the goals of the program, the standard or accepted norms of the institution, or the "way we've always done it," we are acquiring emancipatory knowledge. Becoming a critically reflective teacher has been strongly advocated in recent years (see Brookfield, 1995, for example) and has been linked with the relatively new concept of teaching scholarship (Kreber and Cranton, 2000). This kind of thinking about teaching is emancipatory when it leads us to become open to alternative perspectives.

For each of the examples of communicative knowledge I give, the knowledge becomes emancipatory when we challenge it or critically question the assumptions on which it rests. Why should our university serve the business community? Why do we have these program goals? Why are we putting this course on-line? Why is group process relevant to learning? Do learning styles really matter?

Evaluation of Teaching as Interpretive and Critical

In research, instrumental knowledge is acquired through the empirical-analytical or natural sciences. Quantitative measurement is used. Communicative knowledge is obtained through the hermeneutic or interpretive methodologies. Qualitative data from interviews and conversations, observations, and written materials are used to interpret and understand intersubjective meaning. Emancipatory knowledge is brought about through the critical sciences. The researcher works with co-researcher participants to foster self-reflection, self-development, and joint decision making about possible courses of action.

To assess the *quality* of knowledge within each of these domains, we turn to the same methodologies. The validity of instrumental knowledge is empirically determined; the trustworthiness of communicative knowledge is established through discourse and consensus among informed people. The usefulness of emancipatory knowledge is assessed during critical reflection and challenge by those who participated in creating the knowledge.

If we accept that knowledge about teaching is primarily communicative and emancipatory, then the evaluation of teaching falls into the interpretive and critical paradigms. This means that rather than trying to quantify and objectify perceptions of teaching, as we do when we use student ratings, we accept the process as a subjective one. We do not view subjectivity as something to be overcome. We do not speak of "bias." We realize that different characteristics of teaching are appropriate in different contexts and that students and other people who are viewing, participating in, or assessing teaching are doing so through the lens of their own perspectives on what constitutes good teaching.

To think about the evaluation of teaching in this way may require a paradigm shift, although the recent popularity of teaching portfolios in higher education already demonstrates a shift in our understanding of how we see the evaluation process (see Chapter Three). At least four questions come immediately to mind when we first think about interpretive and critical evaluation:

Have not student ratings (a quantitative measure) been shown to be reliable and valid in decades of research?

How can we rely on qualitative evaluation results that are not likely to be more than a random collection of opinions?

How can we report interpretive results in a concise and meaningful way?

If faculty self-report is included, as it is in the critical paradigm, won't this just be inflated self-promotion?

Student ratings have indeed served us well. They are commonplace at most institutions; they are efficient to administer and relatively easy to interpret. Generally, the research demonstrates their reliability and validity. Although they yield statistical results, student ratings are subjective and interpretive in two crucial ways. First, some person or group (hopefully with a sound knowledge of teaching) selects the items to include on the rating form. In that selection process, the authors of the form are deciding what constitutes good teaching. Second, the students responding to the instrument are doing so based on their personal perception of that class, the social norm regarding teaching that exists in that class or institution, and their prior knowledge and experience with teaching. That they attach ratings or numbers to their perceptions makes them no more objective.

The fact that student ratings are generally reliable and valid is an outcome of at least three factors: (1) the people who create forms agree, more or less, on what should be included; (2) students agree, more or less, on what good teaching is within a specific context; (3) individual differences among student responses are usually statistically removed. We should, by all means, continue to use student ratings of instruction but view them in a different way. We need to keep in mind that they are subjective and interpretive and that they represent only one perspective—a collective perspective where individual voices are lost.

The fear that qualitative evaluation results constitute a random, ungeneralizable, and unrepresentative set of opinions is the same criticism commonly leveled against interpretive research. It is the product of using the criteria from one paradigm to judge work done in another. To interpret does not mean to be random, unfair, or discriminatory. Good interpretive evaluations are trustworthy and credible. They are based on the expertise, professionalism, authenticity, and credibility of the evaluators. There needs to be agreement as to what is being evaluated. Evaluators must be ethical, knowledgeable, caring, responsible, and open-minded. These conditions should not be onerous in a context where we normally engage in peer review, negotiation, and discourse in all aspects of our work.

For people who are used to seeing a short computer-generated summary of student ratings as a representation of the quality of teaching, the longer documents produced by interpretive evaluations can seem time consuming and difficult to wade through. Department chairs or promotion and tenure committees, for example, who have the task of reviewing many teaching evaluations may especially object to qualitative reports. Again, we are using the criteria from one paradigm (concise, parsimonious) to judge the product of another paradigm—one where depth and meaningfulness are considered more important. But in addition to that fundamental contradiction, qualitative evaluation results can be presented in easy-to-read formats. Executive summaries, selected quotes, and a narrative style can make interpretive and critical evaluations more interesting and easier to manage than tables and graphs.

Self-report or self-evaluation is a central component of critical evaluation in particular and is often a part of interpretive evaluation. Faculty may describe their philosophy of practice, comment on student perceptions, or outline their developmental plans. Self-evaluation is often belittled by using the argument that faculty will only describe the good things they do and minimize their weaknesses. Of course, we want to portray ourselves in the best light possible; this is the case in interviews, portfolios, auditions, or any context in which we promote our own work. If the content of the self-report is a description of what we know or believe about teaching, an articulation of our thoughts on teaching, or reflections on our practice, then that *content* can be judged by credible and informed people. Self-evaluation is not simply a matter of a person saying she is "good" and others taking her word for it. Rather, it is a matter of the person demonstrating her knowledge about teaching through writing or talking about it and others assessing the quality of that knowledge.

Interpretive and Critical Strategies for Evaluating Teaching

A wide variety of strategies for interpretive and critical evaluation of teaching are available. Any of the methods used in research can be applied to evaluation. I list several possibilities here, but my suggestions are not exhaustive.

- Classroom observations can be conducted by peers, administrators, or faculty developers. Observations should lead to a qualitative report and should be discussed with the faculty member.
- Peer review of course materials and samples of student work yield information about many facets of teaching.

- Presentations, discussions, or conversations about teaching help us to elaborate on a person's knowledge and experience.
- Interviews of the faculty member and his students or selected student groups may provide a more formal, though not necessarily more structured, way of understanding the person's teaching.
- Letters from students and graduates, solicited or unsolicited, often reveal unusual attributes of someone's teaching.
- In student discussion groups, the students may stimulate each other to come up with comments they may not think of individually.
- In some contexts, reports from employers of students may provide evaluation information.
- Faculty members who do research on teaching and disseminate the results through articles or conference presentations are demonstrating their knowledge about teaching.
- Similarly, faculty who write articles for journals or newsletters on teaching are describing their expertise and experience.
- Reports on innovations in teaching or the innovations themselves (such as a Web-based course) provide evidence for the evaluation of teaching.
- An instructor's contribution to program, curriculum, or course development can be a useful indicator of that person's teaching expertise.
- A philosophy-of-practice statement is becoming a more common part of a curriculum vitae or teaching portfolio.
- In some contexts, reports from the institution's faculty developer on an instructor's involvement in faculty development activities can provide evaluation information.
- A faculty member who initiates faculty development activities (for example, leads workshops or discussion groups) demonstrates her teaching expertise.
- A person who challenges the usual way of doing things in his department or institution (for example, seeks to change grading policies, admission requirements, or standard teaching methods in the program) shows a critically reflective approach to teaching.
- The teaching portfolio is one way in which we can compile and present interpretive and critical evaluation results. It provides an umbrella and an organizational framework for qualitative information (see Chapter Three).

Conclusions

Knowing how to teach is not the same as knowing how to repair an engine or build a shed. When a person repairs an engine, we can objectively judge the quality of the work by measuring how smoothly the engine runs or how much fuel it uses. When a person builds a shed, we can assess whether the construction is straight and stable. Teaching, however, is a specialized form of communication taking place in a social context, with a goal of change in individuals' ways of thinking and knowing. There are no invariant principles. There are no clear, best ways of teaching. Our judgments of the quality of teaching are, by definition, subjective and interpretive.

In the evaluation of teaching, we need to base our strategies on the communicative and emancipatory nature of knowledge about teaching. Our procedures need to be open-ended, qualitative, and flexible. We need to shift our way of thinking about the evaluation of teaching away from attempts to objectify and quantify this complex process of human and social interaction.

References

Brookfield, S. *Becoming a Critically Reflective Teacher*. San Francisco: Jossey-Bass, 1995

Habermas, J. *Knowledge and Human Interests*. Boston: Beacon Press, 1971.

Kreber, C., and Cranton, P. "Exploring the Scholarship of Teaching." *Journal of Higher Education*, 2000, *71*, 476–495.

Mezirow, J. "Transformative Learning: Theory to Practice." In P. Cranton (ed.), *Transformative Learning in Action: Insights from Practice*. New Directions for Adult and Continuing Education, no. 74. San Francisco: Jossey-Bass, 1997.

PATRICIA CRANTON *is professor of adult and higher education at the University of New Brunswick in New Brunswick, Canada.*

3

Portfolios have now been used successfully for almost two decades to document teaching accomplishments and can serve both to stimulate reflection about good practice and to provide evidence for major career decisions.

Using Portfolios to Document Good Teaching: Premises, Purposes, Practices

Christopher Knapper, W. Alan Wright

Although their use in higher education dates back only to the 1980s, teaching portfolios are now found in colleges and universities worldwide. They are being used to document teaching in places as diverse as New Zealand, Sri Lanka, Trinidad, and Hong Kong, as well as the United States and Canada where the concept originated. The underlying idea of portfolios seems self-evident and has long been associated with the fine arts and architecture. People picture a portfolio as a large, slim, zippered, leather case with a carrying handle, brimming with drawings, sketches, portraits, and the like—all designed to demonstrate the professional's talent, expertise, and proficiency. But in fact, the analogy of the teaching portfolio as a collection of "best work" may be rather misleading. As we will see later, an effective portfolio requires selection and organization and must give a rounded picture of teaching ability in order to be convincing for those who read it.

As Knapper (1995) has described, the recent origins of the portfolio can be traced back to the work of a committee of the Canadian Association of University Teachers (CAUT), which was concerned in the 1970s with the undue reliance on student ratings for the evaluation of teaching. This group called for a more broadly based approach to evaluation that would use multiple sources of information and place responsibility for compiling the documentation on the individual faculty member rather than a remote administrator. The committee chair, Bruce Shore, first articulated the idea that faculty members should build their own case for teaching effectiveness—a "portfolio of evidence" to demonstrate competence (Shore, 1975, p. 8). Shortly afterward, the committee set about preparing its *Guide to the*

Teaching Dossier, which was first published in 1980; it appeared in a second edition in 1986 and has been widely emulated and excerpted since then in a variety of publications all over the world (Shore and others, 1980, 1986). In Canada, the concept is still known as the teaching dossier. In the United States, Shore's original term *portfolio* was preferred, perhaps because it had less sinister connotations in the dying days of the Cold War.

The rationale for the teaching portfolio is spelled out clearly in the opening pages of the CAUT *Guide.* It was intended to be a "summary of a professor's major teaching accomplishments and strengths" (Shore and others, 1986, p. 1) in the same way that lists of publications, grants, and academic honors reflect research activity. It would take the form of "selected short descriptions that will accurately convey the scope and quality of the professor's teaching" and "just as statements about research in a CV should be supportable by more complete evidence (for example, published papers or actual research data), so statements made in a teaching dossier should be substantiated by more complete evidence related to teaching activity" (Shore and others, 1986, p. 1).

Some key words here are *accurate, substantiated,* and *evidence.* Although the CAUT committee felt that a portfolio should naturally put forward the best possible case, such a case had to be supportable by evidence in order to be honest, valid, and convincing. In a sense, they were arguing for an approach to documenting good teaching that anticipates the notion of "classroom research" advocated by Cross (1986) and the Boyer-Rice concept of the "scholarship of teaching" (Boyer, 1990). They argue that recording competence and effectiveness in teaching is different from recording research or service, largely because many faculty fail to keep records of what they do as teachers. Many do not recognize the need for taking the initiative and regard the collection of evaluation data as the responsibility of others. "One of the reasons is lack of knowledge of how and what to record" (Shore and others, 1986, p. 3).

Another interesting aspect of the original *Guide* is the recommended length for a portfolio, which the writers felt should be no more than three pages (partly because they envisaged it being incorporated in a traditional vitae). Most teaching portfolios today are much longer than this, though a good case can still be made for limits on length (say around ten pages, excluding appendixes), especially when large numbers of portfolios are being reviewed by a committee or busy administrators.

The *Guide* next outlines the steps needed to create a portfolio, which are still valid and useful. They include clarifying and documenting teaching responsibilities, selecting criteria for effective teaching, compiling evidence in support of those criteria, summarizing the evidence, and collecting exemplary material as back-up if needed.

The longest section of the *Guide* is the one that has been copied most frequently: the famous list of forty-nine categories (or types of evidence) that might be included in a portfolio, grouped under the headings "The products of good teaching" (for example, student work and achievements),

"Material from oneself" (description of teaching duties, course syllabi, instructional innovations, and so on), and "Information from others" (including students, colleagues, alumni, even employers). In other words, the portfolio is seen not as a new *method* of evaluation but rather a *system* for collecting, combining, and organizing information from a wide range of sources, including traditional approaches to teaching evaluations such as peer visits and student ratings. It was envisaged that portfolios would be used mainly for major career decisions such as tenure and promotion, but it was also apparent that compiling a portfolio would stimulate a good deal of reflection about teaching by the individual concerned and by those who read the portfolio.

The Idea Spreads

Although tens of thousands of copies of the *Guide* were distributed, the idea of teaching portfolios was rather slow to take off in Canada, and it was only after the adoption of the concept in the United States that the use of portfolios became widespread. Peter Seldin, who had learned about teaching dossiers at a European conference in 1978, mentioned the idea in his influential 1980 book on teaching evaluation (Seldin, 1980) and later wrote and spoke extensively about portfolios in universities across North America and beyond (see, for example, Seldin, 1991). The American Association for Higher Education (AAHE) convened a national roundtable on portfolios in 1990 and produced one publication relating the concept to the scholarship of teaching (Edgerton, Hutchings, and Quinlan, 1991) and another with accounts of the use of the portfolio throughout the United States (twenty-four institutions) and Canada (one institution) (Anderson, 1993).

Canadians presented the portfolio idea in Australia in the early 1980s through workshops and articles (for example, Knapper, 1981), and in 1987 the Federation of Australian University Staff Associations issued its own guide (Roe, 1987). Portfolios are now widely used through Australia and New Zealand and have indeed been adopted for broader purposes, as Cannon describes in Chapter Nine. In the United Kingdom, the portfolio idea was first presented by Gibbs (1988), who used the term *teaching profile*. Although the exact nature of its use and effectiveness is hard to document, there must be few countries, especially those with Western-style university systems, where teaching portfolios are unknown or untried. In the survey conducted by Wright and O'Neil (1995) of 331 faculty developers in Canada, the United States, Britain, and Australia, participants were asked to rank the use of portfolios as an effective means of improving teaching. The rankings generally fell around the mid-point in a list of thirty-six items and seemed to indicate general familiarity with and acceptance of the portfolio concept.

Organizing a Portfolio

The present chapter is not intended as a practical guide to the preparation of a portfolio; there are many of those (for example O'Neil and Wright, 1995; Knapper and Wilcox, 1998). However, now that portfolios have been used successfully for several years, it is worth summarizing the main components. One way of providing a brief snapshot of what a portfolio looks like is to show a sample table of contents. Exhibit 3.1 shows the main headings a professor of pharmacy used in a portfolio prepared in the early 1990s. More information about this portfolio can be found in O'Neil and Wright, 1995.

This is a fairly comprehensive portfolio—one that closely mirrors the structure recommended in the *Guide*. It is should not be regarded as a template, however, because a key principle of the teaching portfolio is that the content, organization, and presentation are controlled by the individual teacher. There have been attempts in the past to "automate" portfolios by providing fill-in-the-box computerized forms, but this undermines the underlying philosophy of the portfolio approach, which has the advantage of allowing different teachers to tailor a portfolio to their own needs. A portfolio also allows the compiler to provide commentary to help readers interpret what is there—for example to explain gaps or apparent inconsistencies, or even to comment on possibly negative information, such as a poor evaluation by students. At the same time, of course, such commentary must be plausible and not just self-serving, or the whole effort will backfire.

Although each portfolio will be different in both form and content, many commonalities exist. Listed next are the ten most frequently used items, as gathered by Wright from over three hundred faculty at a number of North American colleges and universities (O'Neil and Wright, 1995). Again the data should be regarded as indicative rather than prescriptive.

1. Student course and teaching evaluation data which suggest improvements or produce an overall rating of effectiveness or satisfaction
2. List of course titles and numbers, unit values or credits, enrollments with brief elaboration
3. List of course materials prepared for students
4. Participation in seminars, workshops, and professional meetings intended to improve teaching
5. Statements from colleagues who have observed teaching either as members of a teaching team or as independent observers of a particular course, or who teach other sections of the same course
6. Attempts at instructional innovations and evaluations of their effectiveness
7. Unstructured (and possibly unsolicited) written evaluations by students, including written comments on exams and letters received after a course has been completed

Exhibit 3.1. Table of Contents for a Teaching Portfolio

A. Statement of Teaching Responsibilities
   1. Courses Taught
   2. Student Advising
      individual students
      student committees
   3. Practicums Organized and Supervised
B. Statement of My Teaching Philosophy and Goals
C. Efforts to Improve Teaching
   1. Formal Courses in Education
   2. Conferences Attended
   3. Workshops Attended
   4. Participation in Peer Consultation
D. Redevelopment of Existing Courses
   1. Addition of Tutorials, Role-playing, Case Studies, and so on
   2. Incorporation of Writing Skills
   3. Incorporation of Oral Presentation Skills
   4. Appendix of Representative Course Syllabus and Assignments
E. Information from Students
   1. Summary of Student Ratings
   2. Comments from Student Committees Regarding Advising
F. Service to Teaching
   1. Evaluating Term Papers, Chair
   2. Faculty Evaluation, Co-Chair
   3. Curriculum Committee, Member
   4. Clinical Task Force of Curriculum Committee, Member
G. Information from Colleagues
H. Information from Other Sources
   1. Guest Lectures to Other Faculties
   2. Continuing Education Lectures for Peers
   3. Lectures to Special Interest Groups of the Public
I. Future Teaching Goals

Source: From the portfolio of Professor Margaret Ackman, College of Pharmacy, Dalhousie University.

   8. Participating in course or curriculum development
   9. Evidence of effective supervision on Honors, Master's, or Ph.D. thesis
  10. Student essays, creative work, and projects or field work reports[1]

After many years of reading teaching portfolios and helping many hundreds of faculty to prepare them, we suggest a number of common elements that should almost always be included. First there should be a statement of teaching responsibilities, including details of courses taught, student theses supervised, and service on teaching-related committees (for instance the department curriculum committee). Second is a statement of teaching approach or philosophy, which should reflect underlying teaching principles and include brief examples of how these ideas have been put into practice. Third, data from students, the main "beneficiaries" of teaching (often summaries of student ratings) should be included. We also favor starting with a brief biographical statement to help place the portfolio in context, especially if it is to be a stand-alone document rather than part of a larger vitae. In the case of a faculty member or graduate student at the beginning of a career, it is useful to have a statement of future teaching plans that conveys the idea that the portfolio (and teaching itself) is dynamic, not static. This is the bare bones of a portfolio, and nearly all faculty will be able to include more, in particular evidence of teaching effectiveness from sources other than student ratings, descriptions of teaching innovations, and information about professional development undertaken.

Although more experienced academics will have more evidence in more categories than their junior colleagues, it is important to emphasize that a portfolio should consist of *summaries,* not *raw data.* For example, original course evaluation forms and even multiple testimonials are out of place. In this respect, we might distinguish between the relatively concise portfolio and the larger "portmanteau" containing raw data that can be consulted if necessary (perhaps analogous to the distinction between a tax return and the shoe box used to collect receipts). Some faculty compromise by preparing a fairly short portfolio but attaching appendixes. For summative purposes, this is appropriate within reason, as long as the portfolio alone can stand on its own merits and is short enough to be manageable reading for busy department heads and committee members.

One interesting by-product of embarking on the process of preparing the first portfolio is the realization of how much information is lacking about teaching activities and effectiveness, just as Shore and others (1986) had predicted. In some cases, information that was once available has been lost or discarded; in other cases, it was never collected in the first place. Hence involvement in the portfolio process can be a powerful challenge and impetus to better documentation of teaching processes and outcomes, as Fenwick suggests in Chapter Seven.

Apart from the question of length, one of the most frequent questions raised about portfolios is what span of time they should cover. This depends on the purpose for which the document is to be used, but a good rule of thumb is at least three years—or longer if the teacher is facing a major career decision such as tenure or promotion. But documenting teaching accomplishments from the distant past (say student ratings from six or more years ago) becomes less pertinent as time passes.

Functions and Uses of Portfolios

One difference of opinion about portfolios concerns whether they are most valuable for summative (as originally envisaged by CAUT) or for formative purposes. Further, many proponents of the portfolio approach suggest that an early decision regarding purpose and intended audience is essential, as it will guide and inform the writer's every decision in the portfolio preparation process.

Summative and Formative Uses of Portfolios. It is true that a portfolio intended for a college promotions committee may well take shape quite differently from one intended solely for reflection and teaching improvement purposes. In practice, however, we have found that the differences between the "summative" and the "formative" portfolio are not as great as might be expected. In workshops on portfolio writing for faculty, we habitually ask participants to define their essential purpose as they approach the various tasks. Although a relatively high percentage stress preparation of a document for their tenure and promotion file as the immediate motivation, the resulting documents do not appear to be substantially different from those eventually developed by those tenured professors seeking an avenue to reflection and teaching improvement.

This observation is borne out by the collections of portfolios published regularly since 1995 following Dalhousie University's Annual Recording Teaching Accomplishment Institute. Participants in this intensive, week-long portfolio-writing and consultation process typically express their satisfaction with regard to both the product (the fruits of their five-day effort) and the process, including the workshops, consultations, reflection, writing, and peer mentoring. Goal-oriented participants frequently mention that they were surprised by just how positive and revealing they found the series of encounters with the portfolio experts and colleagues, coupled with the hours of solitary reflection and writing.

In addition to their use for tenure, promotion, and annual performance reviews, portfolios have been employed in the preparation of teaching award files, as a post facto means of articulating an approach to teaching by award winners, as an exemplary document by senior faculty, as a "legacy" document by retiring departmental "builders" or pioneers, as developmental files by graduate teaching assistants, as a part of documentation submitted for a job search, and as a source of evidence for the accreditation of teaching competence (as Beaty describes in Chapter Eight).

In practice, then, the formative and summative purposes of the teaching portfolio merge. Even when prepared largely for summative purposes, the very act of collecting information and interpreting it inevitably leads to self-appraisal and thoughts about possible changes. At the same time, the contents of a portfolio prepared for self-improvement and reflection (for example the material in a statement of teaching philosophy) can be extremely useful to a tenure and promotions committee as an aid to interpreting the results of student evaluations.

Use of Portfolios in Other Contexts. Although the portfolio concept was originally developed to document the teaching accomplishments of individual faculty members, it is has also been used for other purposes and contexts, for example, to document teaching in entire departments and institutions, as Cannon describes in Chapter Nine. Wright and Miller

(2000) describe an educational developer's portfolio, and Knapper (1995) has suggested that portfolios might be used profitably to document university service or even scholarly work, with the aim of broadening the documentation of professional work beyond mere lists so as to show impact.

The Validity of Portfolios

One question frequently raised about portfolios is how valid they are, in particular whether judgments made on the basis of reviewing portfolios are fairer and more accurate than judgments derived from narrower sources of data, such as student ratings. In one sense, portfolios do have face validity simply because they present a fuller picture of teaching than student evaluations alone can provide, with more information and a wider range of sources. In another sense, the lack of a common format for portfolios and the fact that they are compiled by the person being evaluated often leads to suspicion about their reliability and objectivity.

The subject of portfolio evaluation has figured in the literature on portfolios since the early 1990s (Anderson, 1993; Edgerton, Hutchings, and Quinlan, 1991; Seldin, 1993). But formal studies of portfolio procedures, especially those focusing on reliability and validity, are scarce. AAHE described a number of institutional evaluation frameworks in 1993 (Anderson, 1993), ranging from checklists to quantitative models. Canadian guides to the teaching portfolio also provided samples of evaluative procedures (for example, O'Neil and Wright, 1995).

How well, in practice, have faculty aspiring to tenure and promotion been served by their portfolios, as judged by faculty and administrative colleagues? In 1993, Pat Hutchings carried out a major study of American universities using portfolios for the AAHE, and she concluded that they were largely successful.

> Even . . . where portfolios are being used to determine tenure and promotion by committees having little experience with them—judgments have been arrived at, committees have stood behind these decisions, faculty have not flocked to grieve the process. In fact . . . the process of reading and reviewing portfolios has turned out to be illuminating and significant. I hear chairs talking about a better understanding of teaching and learning . . . as a result of reading portfolios. (Anderson, 1993, p. 3)

Although this is encouraging, there are almost no hard data on the success rate of professors who have submitted portfolios for career advancement purposes. Centra (1993) is one of the few researchers to gather data on portfolio reliability and validity. He compared tenure and promotion committee decisions based on portfolios with judgments made without them and found that judgments are reasonably reliable (in the sense of having interjudge agreement), as long as the judges worked from specified criteria. He concluded that using a portfolio for summative decisions about teaching can provide a more complete picture of performance and that evaluation of portfolios can undoubtedly benefit from discussion among evaluators about standards and criteria; he recommended that portfolios should include not only what individuals and others *say* about their teaching but examples of what they actually *do*.

This reflects a common finding that inter-rater reliability in many domains is enhanced when specific criteria are provided and raises the obvious point that, in order to judge effective teaching, there needs to be agreement about just what constitutes effectiveness. We should beware of trying to force portfolios into a quantitative paradigm when one of their strengths is providing rich qualitative data that will be different from person to person. Nonetheless, it is helpful when adopting portfolios to have criteria for judging them that have been discussed and agreed to by members of the teaching community affected, whether at the institutional, school, or departmental level.

One way of doing this has been tried at Queen's University, Ontario, using criteria derived from a statement of effective teaching developed by a university committee. The criteria include *commitment to teaching, teaching load and responsibilities, communication skills, course design and teaching methods, respect for student diversity, involvement in self-evaluation and reflective practice, curriculum development,* and *teaching scholarship.* Those judging portfolios (for example, members of a promotions committee) are provided with a matrix that lists these criteria (with some explanation and amplification) in the left-hand column. In two adjacent columns, they are asked to note first what relevant evidence is contained in the portfolio and second, based on this evidence, how well the teacher meets the criteria. Judges undertake this task independently, then exchange notes. They typically report that having the criteria is extremely useful in helping interpret evidence in portfolios and guiding subsequent discussions.

Conclusions

What can we conclude about the contribution of teaching portfolios to evaluation? First, we can say that they have put more control of the evaluation process into the hands of the individual teacher. Second, teachers are required to take responsibility for documenting teaching accomplishments and finding methods to assess effectiveness of teaching practices. In this sense, as argued earlier, portfolios are quite consistent with ideas underlying classroom research and the scholarship of teaching. Third, portfolios blur the line between summative and formative evaluation. Although they can be used for accountability purposes, to prepare a persuasive teaching portfolio requires both self-evaluation and reflection about personal teaching goals. Fourth, portfolios challenge institutions to develop evaluation processes that are much more sophisticated and broadly based than is pos-sible when relying simply on the results of student ratings. This involves a mutual responsibility on the part of faculty and institutions. On the one hand, faculty must be willing to take the time to document and summarize their teaching accomplishments. On the other hand, faculty colleagues and administrators must ensure that portfolios are taken seriously in the aca-demic rewards process. If evaluation is carried out but no rewards are seen to flow from the process, then there will be little incentive to document teaching or gather evidence for its effectiveness.

References

Anderson, E. (ed.). *Campus Use of the Teaching Portfolio: Twenty-Five Profiles.* Washington, D.C.: American Association for Higher Education, 1993.

Boyer, E. L. *Scholarship Reconsidered: Priorities of the Professoriate.* Princeton, N.J.: Carnegie Foundation for the Advancement of Teaching, 1990.

Centra, J. A. *Reflective Faculty Evaluation: Enhancing Teaching and Determining Faculty Effectiveness.* San Francisco: Jossey-Bass, 1993.

Cross, K. P. "A Proposal to Improve Teaching or What 'Taking Teaching Seriously' Should Mean." *American Association for Higher Education Bulletin,* 1986, 39(1), 9–14.

Edgerton, R., Hutchings, P., and Quinlan, K. *The Teaching Portfolio. Capturing the Scholarship in Teaching.* Washington, D C.: American Association for Higher Education, 1991.

Gibbs, G. *Creating a Teaching Profile.* Bristol, England: Teaching and Educational Services, 1988.

Knapper, C. K. "Evaluating University Instruction: The Teaching Dossier." *HERDSA News,* Nov. 1981, pp. 5–7.

Knapper, C. K. "The Origins of Teaching Portfolios." *Journal on Excellence in College Teaching,* 1995, 6(1), 45–56.

Knapper, C. K., and Wilcox, S. *Preparing a Teaching Dossier.* Kingston, Canada: Queen's University Instructional Development Centre, 1998.

O'Neil, C., and Wright, W. A. *Recording Teaching Accomplishment: A Dalhousie Guide to the Teaching Dossier.* (5th ed) Halifax, Canada: Dalhousie University Office of Instructional Development and Technology, 1995.

Roe, E. *How to Compile a Teaching Portfolio.* Kensington, Australia: Federation of Australian University Staff Associations, 1987.

Seldin, P. *Successful Faculty Evaluation Programs: A Practical Guide to Improve Faculty Performance and Promotion/Tenure Decisions.* Crugers, N.Y.: Coventry Press, 1980.

Seldin, P. *The Teaching Portfolio: A Practical Guide to Improved Performance and Promotion/Tenure Decisions.* Bolton, Mass.: Anker, 1991.

Seldin, P., and Associates. *Successful Use of Teaching Portfolios.* Bolton, Mass.: Anker, 1993.

Shore, B. M. "Moving beyond the Course Evaluation Questionnaire in Evaluating University Teaching." *CAUT Bulletin,* 1975, 23(4), 7–10.

Shore, B. M., and Associates. *The Teaching Dossier: A Guide to its Preparation and Use.* Ottawa: Canadian Association of University Teachers, 1980.

Shore, B. M., and Associates. *The Teaching Dossier: A Guide to its Preparation and Use.* (rev. ed.) Ottawa: Canadian Association of University Teachers, 1986.

Wright, W. A., and O'Neil, M. C. "Teaching Improvement Practices: International

Perspectives." In W. A. Wright and Associates, *Teaching Improvement Practices: Successful Strategies for Higher Education*, pp. 1–57. Bolton, Mass.: Anker, 1995.

Wright, W. A., and Miller, J. A. "The Educational Developer's Portfolio." *International Journal for Academic Development*, 2000, 5, 20–29.

W. ALAN WRIGHT is director of instructional development and technology at Dalhousie University in Halifax, Nova Scotia.

CHRISTOPHER KNAPPER is director of the Instructional Development Centre at Queen's University, Ontario.

4

*Teaching awards act as an implicit evaluation process.
Analyzing our institutional teaching awards according to
Menges's framework allows us to understand the
strengths and weaknesses of the process.*

Evaluating Teaching Through Teaching Awards

Ellen Carusetta

When we think of teaching awards, we do not automatically think of the evaluation of teaching. Yet that is what we do when we bestow teaching awards; we use a set of criteria to judge who we believe are exemplary teachers. It has long been accepted that teaching awards are a standard way for institutions of higher education to honor teaching. Sorcinelli and Davis (1996) suggest that one of the earliest teaching awards may have been given at the University of California in 1959. Research indicates that in the United States close to 70 percent of two-year colleges and liberal arts institutions and 96 percent of research universities surveyed have awards or programs honoring exemplary teaching (Crawley, 1995; Jenrette and Hayes, 1996; Menges, 1996; Zahorski, 1996).

In this chapter, I review the literature on teaching awards and then examine a specific case study: the Alan P. Stuart Award for Excellence in Teaching at the University of New Brunswick (UNB), using Menges's three tests of effective awards.

Overview of Awards Processes

Teaching awards have not received much attention in the literature. Authors describe different award programs, discuss the effectiveness of awards in motivating faculty to improve teaching, and examine the process of giving teaching awards. Much of the literature is expository rather than research-based. I concentrate on the effectiveness of and processes surrounding teaching awards.

Effectiveness. The literature on the effectiveness of teaching awards runs the gamut from those who believe teaching awards are in and of themselves a good thing to those who are not supportive of them. Some authors believe that when good teaching is rewarded, faculty will remain committed to the improvement of teaching. Seldin (1999) states that "administrators who recognize and reward improvement in teaching will be able to sustain an ongoing program of evaluation that results in teaching improvement" (p. 205). Wright (1995) refers to Rice and Austin (1990), and Sorcinelli (1986), as authors who believe formal awards for teaching can serve as strong incentives. Kaikai and Kaikai (1990) state that recognizing and rewarding excellence in teaching can help relieve teacher burnout.

At the other end of the spectrum are those who believe that institutional rewards by themselves have little or no effect on the improvement of teaching. Research by Ruedrich, Cavey, Katz, and Grush (1992) and by Ruedrich, Reid, and Chu (1986) shows that teaching awards do not act as incentives for improvement but are effective as a method of recognizing and rewarding effective teaching. Zahorski (1996) suggests that individual teaching awards can be a detriment to encouraging teaching as a collaborative and cooperative activity. Ward (1995) considers institutional awards a neutral force for improving teaching, and Forsythe and Gandolfo (1996) go so far as to say that if teaching is valued in the institutional culture, then teaching awards are irrelevant. Finally, McNaught and Anwyl (1993), in a survey of thirty-seven Australian institutions of higher education, report: "Recognizing distinguished teaching achievement is highly laudable in itself; however, it is highly arguable whether instituting teaching awards will produce behavioural changes in sundry other academics or promote overall excellence in an institution" (p. 20).

Most authors hold the middle ground that teaching awards are effective when they are representative of an institutional culture that values good teaching and when they are part of a program designed to encourage teaching effectiveness. According to Weimer (1991), "Teaching awards work successfully when they represent one of many ways in which instructional excellence and efforts to achieve it are recognized, valued, and rewarded" (p. 136). Centra (1993), Knapper (1997), Menges (1996), and Sorcinelli and Davis (1996) echo these sentiments and call for a strong network of incentives and rewards for teaching to be a positive part of the institutional climate and values.

One observation I made while reviewing literature is that teaching awards are often not mentioned in a discussion of other rewards in higher education. The book by Braskamp and Ory (1994) on assessing faculty work mentions, in only one paragraph, the honor and recognition one receives both in and outside the institution with the receipt of any award. Marchant and Newman (1994) interviewed heads of 245 departments of educations in U.S. colleges and universities to ask their opinions about faculty activities and reward procedures, and there is no record of teaching awards being mentioned. Diamond (1993) and Diamond and Adam (1993) discuss the need to change priorities in the faculty reward system and offer suggestions on how administrators can effect change in the way teaching is viewed in the tenure and promotion process, but teaching awards were not a part of this discussion.

Administration. Many authors have looked at the process of administering teaching awards and offer suggestions on how it might be improved. McNaught and Anwyl (1993) state that teaching awards would be better if they emphasized the cooperative nature of teaching; if they were a means to provide adequate support for innovation in teaching; if they emphasized the interplay between teaching, research, and community service; and if we limit claims about what they are likely to do. Seldin (1990) states that teaching is pitted against research and that, in order to counter this, recipients for teaching awards should be individuals who are respected for their research as well.

Teaching awards have been used in research as a means of determining the attributes of exemplary teachers. Award winners have been interviewed to examine factors such as creativity (Trunnell, Evans, Richards, and Grosshans, 1997), and nomination letters have been examined through content analyses to determine how faculty and students define excellence in teaching (Donaldson, 1988; Goldsmith, Gruber, and Wilson 1977; Lowman, 1996).

Part of the literature focuses on the mystique that seems to surround teaching awards and advocates that a clear and visible set of procedures be required to dispel some of the problems with them. Knapper's perception after twenty years of administering teaching awards is that "the procedures for selecting the awardees can be erratic" (Knapper, 1997, p. 45). Menges states that "vagueness and secrecy foster suspicions about the objectivity and accuracy of the selection process" (Menges, 1996, p. 4). According to Edgerton (1993), concerns about teaching awards center on whether or not merit prevails in the selection process. Meredith (1990) offers procedures for evaluating the dossiers submitted by award nominees. And finally, Weimer states that the problem with teaching awards is that they "smack of tokenism" (Weimer, 1991, p. 135), which is a result of the policies, practices, and procedures that surround the awards.

Svinicki and Menges (1996) offer suggestions on how awards should be structured, describe the settings for teaching awards at different institutions, and discuss ways other than teaching awards through which exemplary teachers can be identified. In their book, a chapter by Menges describes three tests to determine the effectiveness of teaching awards: (1) the selection validity test, (2) the faculty motivation test, and (3) the test of public perceptions. I use the UNB Stuart Award as a case study to illustrate deconstructing teaching awards.

Case Study: The Stuart Award

As acting coordinator of the Teaching and Learning Centre (TLC) at UNB, one of my responsibilities was to administer the Alan P. Stuart Award for Excellence in Teaching. The TLC was assigned this duty by the office of the Vice-President Academic, from whose office it had previously been administered.

I use the word *administer* twice in the previous paragraph; as I read it over, my first inclination was to change this verb. But even though it is not a word that sits easily with me, it is the right one. It is my perception that the Stuart Award was conceived of as yet another administrative duty for the vice president's office. This is not to say that it was not considered important but rather, with the excessive work of the VP's office, the process encompassing the Stuart Award may not have been given the critical consideration it needed. When the TLC was assigned this duty, I wanted to be confident that the Stuart Award truly honored distinguished teaching performance. At that time it was our one institutional award to celebrate teaching—our one chance to show the university community that we value good teaching.

The first of Menges's three tests is the "selection validity test," which seeks to understand how well the program rewards truly outstanding teachers. Selection must be accurate and representative. Accuracy is determined through five indicators and representativeness through three. Menges's criteria, to a great extent, mirror the criteria one would look for in an effective evaluation process.

Reflection of Mission.   First, to be accurate the program must reflect the core values of the institution. The UNB mission statement mentions teaching twice: UNB (1) "strives to be known for its excellence in teaching by providing students with the highest possible quality instruction" and (2) ". . . to encourage the development of a network of international cooperation in teaching, research, and community development." The Stuart Award easily fits within this broad, nonrestrictive statement.

The second indicator of accuracy is reflected in whether faculty are aware of the criteria and procedures for the award and if these are perceived to be correct. As the initial set of criteria for the Stuart Award are stated on the nomination form, they are known. Whether or not they are considered correct is difficult to tell. We do know that the criteria were based on previous research on what constitutes good teaching and that no one has complained about the criteria. I do not think faculty are aware of the second set of criteria or the procedures used to determine the award winners. This is an area that is addressed in the literature as a problem and that needs, as Menges states, to be free of vagueness and suspicion. In any evaluative process, it is important that those being evaluated understand the criteria used (Brookfield, 1990).

Third, selection must use information of various types and from several sources. It is important in any evaluation process, whether it be of learning or teaching, that different sources of evaluation be used to gain a complete picture. The initial shortlist for the Stuart Award is compiled from all complete nominations. For a nomination to be complete, a letter of support must accompany it. Usually, only those with more than one letter of support and those who have been nominated in previous years are shortlisted. The nomination letters and the nominee's portfolio provide multiple sources of information, but there are problems with both.

The nomination form itself is problematic. It identifies instructors only by their name, their campus, and the term in which they taught. There is no place to identify the course. The constitution of the class can affect a student's perception of the instructor and should be considered. For example, an instructor working with an upper-level, small class is likely to be considered in a more favorable light than one working with an introductory course with hundreds of participants (Marsh, 1987).

Using a Likert-type scale to support nominations seems rather redundant. All nominees are given an "A" grade for each of the criteria. In 1999, sixty-five nominations were received; however, only twenty-four of these were considered complete in that the nomination forms were accompanied by at least one letter of support. As the qualitative information in a letter is more meaningful than the ineffective Likert-type scale, the scale could be replaced with a more qualitative format that asks nominees to comment on each of the criteria. Nominees could also be advised to write an accompanying letter to address other qualities they think are important but are not represented in the eight criteria.

When instructors are informed that they are on the shortlist for the Stuart Award, they are given a very short period of time to submit a teaching portfolio. In a perfect world, all instructors would have this readily available. But not one of the nominees we contacted had an up-to-date portfolio available.

The portfolios we did receive varied in content and quality. Nominees must have access to information on what to include in portfolios and be given enough time to put together a good one. A faculty development center should be available to offer professional advice in this area. The TLC has been working on a portfolio template for the Web that would give nominees the information they need to develop a comprehensive portfolio. This would also assist the committee in their deliberations, because portfolios that follow similar guidelines would be easier to assess. This comes back to the idea that in a fair evaluation, the criteria should be explicit and the playing field as level as possible.

The fourth and fifth indicators can be addressed together: Are nominees considered for their future teaching plans as well as their past accomplishments, and how confident are those who make the selections that recipients are superior in terms of program criteria? These indicators are difficult to assess in this case study, because committee members do not meet until the final choice is made. Each committee member functions independently and is not required to justify his or her choices. I found it peculiar that one nominee advanced to the final shortlist after submitting a portfolio that simply consisted of student rating forms for the past several years. Committees need to communicate with each other.

Degree of Representativeness. The first criterion in this area is whether recipients fairly represent a variety of fields and instructional situations.

Simple calculations of the nominations for the Stuart Award indicate that females tend to nominate instructors almost twice as often as males. Instructors from a majority of fields were represented, although the arts and the professional faculties did garner the majority of the nominations. There were only two nominations from the sciences. It is obvious that not all fields are equally represented, and it is difficult to know the repercussions of the majority of nominations coming from females.

The second criterion addresses whether recipients represent the variety of instructional activities that faculty perform both in and out of class. How an instructor actually teaches is not one of the explicit criteria for the Stuart Award. I do not believe the committee goes out of its way to reward different types of instruction, nor do I perceive this to be a problem. There seems to be an acceptance that good teaching can happen in any instructional setting and that exemplary teachers can employ any number of different teaching techniques. The only mention of how instructors interact outside the classroom is through the criterion of whether instructors are available to students outside of class.

Third, Menges suggests that programs need to be free of gender and ethnic bias. Such bias does not appear to be a problem with the Stuart Award. A sense of fairness seems pervasive in the process. As UNB has two campuses (one in Fredericton and one in Saint John), there is an understanding that the award should be given to one instructor at each campus, a practice that often occurs.

Student nominations are valued above nominations by colleagues. Although most nominations are from students, and this is one of the criteria to be considered, there are some very good nominations from colleagues. No one on the committee shortlisted any of these persons. Nominations from colleagues seem to be met with some scepticism. Were they submitted to help a colleague in the tenure and promotion process? Student nominations are trusted; they seem to be void of ulterior motives.

Other unwritten biases include full- or part-time instructors, gender, and length of service to the university. In the final deliberations for the Stuart Award, when the committee met it became evident that full-time instructors are given priority over part-time instructors. Committee members also commented on the appropriateness of having one male and one female award winner, as well as one fairly early in his career with another near the end. These and any other biases that may exist need to be discussed and made explicit. It is important in any evaluative practice that the evaluators understand any assumptions they may hold.

Test of Motivation. Menges states that a good award program should energize faculty and make them more attentive to their teaching. Two criteria are addressed: (1) ensuring incentive value and (2) giving evidence of an increase in motivation.

Ensuring Incentive Value. The first indicator of this criterion is whether the awards are sufficiently numerous to encourage qualified faculty to apply.

As faculty need to be nominated for the Stuart Award, this indicator is only partially relevant. If one were to look at the number of awards given (two) in relation to the number of faculty (approximately 780) at UNB, the odds are not very high. Until this year, the Stuart Award was the only institutional award for teaching.

The second indicator—whether there is a menu of awards to choose from—is becoming a reality. UNB is putting two other awards into place.

The third indicator asks whether the value of the award is at least as great as the effort required to obtain it. Because there is no extrinsic value to the Stuart Award, this is difficult to ascertain. Most authors state that the value in these awards is often intrinsic (Seldin, 1999; Weimer, 1991). This would have to be the case with the Stuart Award.

The final indicator of this criterion is whether or not unsuccessful nominees receive feedback telling them how their application could be strengthened. At UNB those who submit portfolios receive no feedback. According to Zubizarreta (1999), "the teaching portfolio emerges as one compelling solution to the need for professors to evaluate rigorously and improve systematically standards for teaching and learning . . . it can serve as a compelling structure for comprehensive review" (p. 180). Receiving feedback is an important part of the process.

Evidence of Increase in Motivation. The first indicator asks if nomination rates are increasing for the award. With the transfer of responsibility for the Stuart Award to the TLC, only data from the past three years are available to scrutinize. According to the administrative assistant of the TLC, nomination rates have declined over the past few years. It would be difficult to know why this is so; our faculty complement has remained fairly constant in the past few years, and nomination procedures have not changed.

Second, evidence of increasing motivation can be found if recipients report positive experiences in the wake of receiving the award. Recipients receive the Stuart Award at convocation, are asked to write a paper for the TLC newsletter, are interviewed for press releases, and are contacted by the TLC for permission to put their names forward for regional or national awards. If positive experiences were defined to include such activities as seminars and workshops, we could further promote effective teaching by having award winners give workshops and in other ways champion the cause of teaching at UNB.

The four remaining indicators (Has informal conversation about teaching increased? Do agendas of departments and committees contain more teaching-related items? Are instructional experiments and innovations more common? and Have student course and teacher evaluations become more positive?) are items that can be addressed together. Although the TLC has reported increasing interest in their sessions on teaching, there is no indication that this is motivated by the Stuart Award. To determine this, institutions would need to survey faculty.

Test of Public Perceptions. The final test is one of whether external audiences have an increased awareness that teaching is valued and that it is improved. The four indicators are as follows: (1) Is media coverage more extensive and more positive? (2) When prospective students and their parents ask questions about the quality of teaching, are these questions easily answered? (3) When legislators ask questions about such things as faculty workload, are their questions better informed? (4) Has external funding for the support of instructional innovation increased?

Many factors can affect each of these indicators. At UNB there is media coverage for the award, but it has not changed over the years. Award winners are noted in the UNB newsletter, and news releases are sent out to the Fredericton newspaper and the student newspaper. It is interesting that the Saint John paper does not accept the releases. Without conducting some research, it would be difficult to determine whether students and parents get better answers to their questions or whether legislators ask better questions. Finally, external funding for instructional innovation has increased, but I would not think it is due to our awards program. Monies have been received from a foundation to set up a bachelor's degree in leadership, but most of the external funds received recently have been to promote technology and distance education. It would be a hard stretch to link these to the Stuart Award.

Conclusion

Bestowing a teaching award is an evaluative process. Analyzing our institutional awards according to Menges's framework allows us to understand the strengths and weaknesses of the process. The Stuart Award fares well in the selection validity test but falls short in the faculty motivation and the public perception tests. The process itself needs to be more transparent to the university community and collaborative among those who make the selections. The criteria used need to be open and explicit both for the nominees and the evaluators. The nominees need more support in putting their applications together, and public perception of the award and its value to the university needs to be bolstered. Following Menges's framework could make this award a valuable evaluative process.

References

Braskamp, L. A., and Ory, J. C. *Assessing Faculty Work.* San Francisco: Jossey-Bass, 1994.

Brookfield, S. *The Skillful Teacher.* San Francisco: Jossey-Bass, 1990.

Centra, J. A. *Reflective Faculty Evaluation.* San Francisco: Jossey-Bass, 1993.

Crawley, A. L. "Faculty Development Programs at Research Universities: Implications for Senior Faculty Renewal." In E. Neal (ed.), *To Improve the Academy,* 1995, 14, 1995.

Diamond, R M. "Instituting Change in the Faculty Reward System." In R. M. Diamond and B. E. Adam (eds.), *Recognizing Faculty Work: Reward Systems for the Year 2000.* New Directions for Higher Education, no. 81. San Francisco: Jossey-Bass, 1993.

Diamond R. M , and Adam, B. E. "Changing Priorities and the Faculty Reward System." In R. M. Diamond and B. E. Adam (eds.), *Recognizing Faculty Work: Reward Systems for the Year 2000.* New Directions for Higher Education, no. 81. San Francisco: Jossey-Bass, 1993.

Donaldson, J. F. "Exemplary Instruction of Adults: The Case of an Excellence in Off-Campus Teaching Award, Part II." *Journal of Continuing Higher Education,* 1988, *36*(2), 11–18.

Edgerton, R. "The Re-Examination of Faculty Priorities." *Change,* 1993, *25*(4), 10–25.

Forsythe, G. B., and Gandolfo, A. "Promoting Exemplary Teaching: The Case of the U.S. Military Academy." In M. D. Svinicki and R. J. Menges (eds.), *Honoring Exemplary Teaching.* New Directions for Teaching and Learning, no. 65. San Francisco: Jossey-Bass, 1996.

Goldsmith, C. A., Gruber, J. E., and Wilson, K. E. "Perceived Attributes of Superior Teachers: An Inquiry into the Giving of Teacher Awards." *American Educational Research Journal,* 1977, *14,* 423–440.

Jenrette, M., and Hayes, K. "Honoring Exemplary Teaching: The Two-Year College Setting." In M. D. Svinicki and R. J. Menges (eds.), *Honoring Exemplary Teaching.* New Directions for Teaching and Learning, no. 65. San Francisco: Jossey-Bass, 1996.

Kaikai, S., and Kaikai, R. "Positive Ways to Avoid Instructor Burnout." Paper presented at the National Conference on Successful College Teaching, Orlando, Fla., Feb. 28-Mar. 3, 1990. (ED 320 623)

Knapper, C. "Rewards for Teaching." In P. Cranton (ed.), *University Challenges in Faculty Work: Fresh Perspectives from Around the World.* New Directions for Teaching and Learning, no. 65. San Francisco: Jossey-Bass, 1997.

Lowman, J. "Characteristics of Exemplary Teachers." In M. D. Svinicki and R. J. Menges (eds.), *Honoring Exemplary Teaching.* New Directions for Teaching and Learning, no. 65. San Francisco: Jossey-Bass, 1996.

Marchant, G., and Newman, I. "Faculty Activities and Rewards: Views from Education Administrators in the USA." *Assessment and Evaluation in Higher Education,* 1994, *19,* 145–153.

Marsh, H. W. "Student Evaluations of University Teaching: Research Findings, Methodological Issues, and Directions for Future Research." *International Journal of Educational Research,* 1987, *11,* 253–288

McNaught, C., and Anwyl, J. "Awards for Teaching Excellence at Australian Universities." University of Melbourne Centre for the Study of Higher Education Research Working Paper no. 93.1, 1993. (ED 368 291)

Menges, R. J. "Awards to Individuals." In M. D. Svinicki and R. J. Menges (eds.), *Honoring Exemplary Teaching.* New Directions for Teaching and Learning, no. 65. San Francisco: Jossey-Bass, 1996.

Meredith, G. M. "Dossier Evaluation for Screening Candidates for Excellence in Teaching Awards." *Psychological Reports,* 1990, *67,* 879–882.

Rice, R. E., and Austin, A. E. "Organizational Impacts of Faculty Morale and Motivation to Teach." In P. Seldin and Associates (eds.), *How Administrators Can Improve Teaching.* San Francisco: Jossey-Bass, 1990, 23–42.

Ruedrich, S. L., Cavey, C., Katz, K., and Grush, L. "Recognition of Teaching Excellence through the Use of Teaching Awards: A Faculty Perspective." *Academic Psychiatry,* 1992, *16*(1), 10–13.

Ruedrich, S., Reid, W., and Chu, C. "Rewarding Teaching Excellence with Cash: A Faculty Response." *Psychiatric Annals,* 1986, *16*(6), 370–373

Seldin, P., and Associates. *How Administrators Can Improve Teaching: Moving from Talk to Action in Higher Education.* San Francisco: Jossey-Bass, 1990.

Seldin, P. *Changing Practices in Evaluating Teaching.* Boulton, Mass.: Anker, 1999.

Sorcinelli, M. D. "Tracing Academic Career Paths: Implications for Faculty Development." *To Improve the Academy,* 1986, *5,* 169–181.

Sorcinelli, M. D., and Davis, B. G. "Honoring Exemplary Teachers in Research Universities." In M. D. Svinicki and R. J. Menges (eds.), *Honoring Exemplary Teaching.* New Directions for Teaching and Learning, no. 65. San Francisco: Jossey-Bass, 1996.

Svinicki, M. D., and Menges, R. J. (eds.). *Honoring Exemplary Teaching.* New Directions for Teaching and Learning, no. 65. San Francisco: Jossey-Bass, 1996.

Trunnell, E., Evans, C., Richards, B., and Grosshans, O. "Factors Associated with Creativity in Health Educators who Have Won Teaching Awards: A Modified Qualitative Approach." *Journal of Health Education,* 1997, *28*(1), 35–41.

Ward, B. "Improving Teaching across the Academy: Gleanings from Research." In E. Neal (ed.), *To Improve the Academy,* 1995, *14*, 27–42.

Weimer, M. E. *Improving College Teaching.* San Francisco: Jossey-Bass, 1991.

Wright, A. W., and Associates. *Teaching Improvement Practices: Successful Strategies for Higher Education.* Boulton, Mass.: Anker, 1995.

Zahorski, K. J. "Honoring Exemplary Teaching in the Liberal Arts Institution." In M. D. Svinicki and R. J. Menges (eds.), *Honoring Exemplary Teaching.* New Directions for Teaching and Learning, no. 65. San Francisco: Jossey-Bass, 1996.

Zubizarreta, J. "Evaluating Teaching through Portfolios." In P. Seldin, (ed.), *Changing Practices in Evaluating Teaching.* Boulton, Mass.: Anker, 1999.

ELLEN CARUSETTA is associate professor of education at the University of New Brunswick in New Brunswick, Canada.

5

*The temptation to use new technologies to streamline
evaluation processes is strong. In this chapter, we provide
a balanced view, based on the classic design proposition
that form follows function and suggest applications of
technology that hold promise for improving evaluation
practice.*

Using Technology to Facilitate Evaluation

Michael Theall, Jennifer Franklin

The promise of new technologies has always been "faster, better, cheaper."
Whether in industry, education, or daily life, the dictum of the past century
has been to use technology to improve efficiency, speed, productivity, and
even quality of life. Many once-fanciful dreams have become reality. Jules
Verne described a fantastic vehicle capable of traveling thousands of leagues
under the sea, and he began his trip "from the earth to the moon" at a location now called Cape Canaveral. Gadgets like comic strip detective Dick
Tracy's two-way wrist radio (later updated to a two-way wrist TV) and
Captain Kirk's Star Trek communicator have become the cell phones,
pagers, and palm computers of our day. Fiber optics, streamed video,
immense capacity for data storage, retrieval, and analysis, and instant communication beckon us to a future of immediacy and convenience. We have
seen the "third wave" and are embarking on yet another. Each of these rev-
olutions has been heralded by the same promises.

Technology and Teaching: The Gutenberg Debate and More

In education, the radical departure from tutorials to the available printed
word was viewed with suspicion. In the last century, after four hundred
years of print, have we leapt from books and blackboards to on-line courses
and degree programs and the promise of the various new technologies. That
promise, from film to radio to programmed instruction booklets to television and now to computers, has always been the same: students would learn
more, learn faster, and learn better. The threat of these new technologies

has been that they would somehow cheapen education and learning. They would make it impersonal and, like books, reduce the importance and power of the teacher. Hundreds of essentially similar studies were conducted to compare "traditional" instruction to instruction that employed technology.

The reality has been considerably different than the promise. Studies from the review by Chu and Schramm (1967) of television research to the outline by Russell (1999) of 355 studies of computer-based and distance instruction have reached essentially the same conclusion: that while technology has the potential to provide powerful teaching and learning tools, in itself and in the absence of well-conceptualized and designed instruction, it is simply a conduit, ultimately no more beneficial than or different from the printed page. Without the teacher to construct meaningful experiences and situations and to integrate information, application, analysis, synthesis, evaluation, and reflection, the technology is only a passive conductor. Chu and Schramm note two overriding questions: "(1) does the situation call for it? and (2) how, in the given situation, can it be used effectively?" (p. 98).

Now that systems, software, and support resources are in place (see, for example, Green, 1999), the question has extended from the use of technology in teaching and learning to the use of technology as a tool for collecting, managing, storing, analyzing, and reporting evaluation data. The existence of infrastructures for other purposes has led to some bold proposals about the efficiency and effectiveness of technology-based evaluation for both formative and summative purposes (for example, by Hmieleski and Champagne, 2000). These proposals have also been seriously questioned, for example, by Theall (2000), who has claimed there is little evidence for the superiority of technology-based systems and there may be dangers in overestimating the capabilities of technology without a realistic assessment of all the other underlying factors that are critical to comprehensive evaluation systems (Arreola, 2000; Theall and Franklin, 1990b).

Examples of Current Activity

There have been many efforts to incorporate technology into evaluation practice, and scores of higher education institutions have experimented with processes for data collection, analysis, and reporting, as well as wrestling with issues related to confidentiality, security, and system management. One of the most coherent multi-institution projects has been the work undertaken by several universities in Hong Kong and in neighboring Southeast Asian countries. Reports of these efforts (Balasubramanian, 1999; Ha, 2001; Lo, Wong, Barrett, and technology to evaluation (Ha and Marsh, 1999; Mah, 2001; Ng, 2001; Olubbemiro, 2001; Shah and Lo, 2001), quality management (Lai-kuen and Kamel, 1999a), student-teacher communication (Lai-kuen and Kamel, 1999b), data collection (Balcombe, 1999), and on-line utilities for questionnaire construction (Lo, Wong, Barrett, and Wong, 1999a) have addressed the applications of Wong, 1999b).

Mechanisms for data collection, analysis, and reporting are quite sophisticated; in fact, Ha and Marsh (1999) have shown that response rates and response distributions are very similar for on-line evaluation and questionnaires distributed in the traditional format. However, Theall (2000) has raised concerns about the extent to which some systems meet the underlying criteria for good evaluation practice.

The Hong Kong experience and that of North American and United Kingdom higher education raises questions about the use of computing technology and the World Wide Web. The dialogue centers around four important issues:

1. *What evaluation issues and concerns must be addressed before technological issues are brought into the discussion?* It's still evaluation, whether or not technology is used and, considering the functions of the process, technology choices should be secondary to decisions based on good evaluation practice.
2. *What technologies can be effectively and efficiently used for data management and other evaluation processes?* Given the first item, the answer has to be that the technologies must provide the functionality required by best practice and the contextual particulars involved.
3. *What security, confidentiality, and legal issues are involved?* Clearly, data security, protection from unauthorized intrusions, and confidentiality are critical. Other concerns center on quality control and the appropriate analysis, reporting, and distribution of results, given the mechanized nature of on-line evaluation.
4. *How can the integrity, value, and dependability of the systems be monitored and maintained?* The evaluation of evaluation systems themselves is often overlooked in both paper and on-line systems. Is responsibility appropriately assigned to qualified professionals? Is there monitoring of the system's psychometric, technical, and logistical performance? Are regular cycles of revalidation and revision part of the overall process?

Under certain circumstances (for example, with poorly designed processes and instruments), we cannot expect any differences between paper and electronic evaluation. Both will be poor, and indeed the immediacy and speed of the electronic format raises the question of whether electronic evaluation can only do a bad job faster. However, when embedded in a truly comprehensive system and when designed specifically to accomplish evaluation objectives, computing technologies can provide unique capabilities. The major question is whether the practical gains are sufficient to justify the widespread adoption of on-line evaluation.

In the remainder of this chapter, we address the questions just posed. We outline important underlying considerations for valid, reliable, accurate, useful, and defensible evaluation, and we demonstrate how systems can be developed that capitalize on the power of technology to provide meaningful and useful information with maximum efficiency and minimum risk.

Laying the Foundation

In our previous writing on evaluation (Franklin and Theall, 1989, 1990; Theall and Franklin, 1990a, 1990b, 1991a, 1991b), we have emphasized day-to-day practice and appropriate formative and summative use of the data as factors even more critical than the psychometric qualities of evaluation data in general or the specific instruments used. We have done this because we believe that operational practice, that is the policies, process, and procedures used, determine to a great extent whether evaluation will succeed, be ignored, or fail.

We advocate building a real "system" for evaluation, not an ad hoc and unsystematic process. The following are some important guidelines (from Theall, 2000) for effective evaluation that are independent of the technologies used. Most of these guidelines are especially relevant to the use of student ratings.

- Consult authoritative sources on the process of developing and operating a comprehensive evaluation system.
- Establish the purpose of the evaluation and the uses and users of ratings beforehand.
- Include all stakeholders in decisions about evaluation process and policy, keeping a balance between individual and institutional needs.
- Publicly present clear information about the evaluation criteria, process, and procedures.
- Establish a legally defensible process and a system for grievances.
- Absolutely include resources for improvement and support of teaching and teachers.
- Use, adapt, or develop instrumentation suited to institutional and individual needs.
- Use multiple sources of information from several situations.
- Archive all ratings data and validate the instruments used.
- Produce reports that can be easily and accurately understood.
- Educate the users of ratings results to avoid misuse and misinterpretation.
- Keep formative evaluation confidential and separate from summative decision making.
- In summative decisions, make direct comparisons among teachers only on the basis of data from similar instructional situations and with consideration of the statistical limitations of ratings data.
- Consider the appropriate use of evaluation data for assessment and other purposes. For example, use aggregate, anonymous data in institutional research on student satisfaction, teaching and learning issues, and learning outcomes.

Given a carefully developed set of policies and a shared understanding of the intents and purposes of the evaluation process, questions about the methods and technologies used can then be addressed. For example, in a system that serves both formative and summative purposes, there is a need to administer, process, and analyze different questionnaires at different times and also to produce reports that contain formative or summative information or both. Different campus units down to the department level may use different forms that nonetheless contain identical institutional, college, school, or even department core items, as well as unique items.

The potential complexities of such processes require sophisticated data management capabilities. Timely analysis, reporting, and the return of results demand efficient and rapid systems. Only the newer computing technologies can offer the power to perform all these complex tasks within a short time while maintaining data integrity. In the following sections, we describe the evolution of a system that was designed with multifunctionality in mind and has performed effectively in a number of high-volume higher-education settings. Finally, we offer guidelines for the development of organizational and technological infrastructures that support this multifunctional evaluation.

Highlights from the Development and Evolution of a Teacher-Course Evaluation (TCE) System

TCE-Tools is the current incarnation of a teacher-course evaluation database management and delivery system that has evolved over more than seventeen years across eight institutions. Designed to support both formative and summative evaluation from the same set of organizational resources, it consists of a dedicated database management system and a suite of student ratings questionnaires and reports tailored to different evaluative purposes (formative and summative) and different instructional settings (for example, lecture, lab, studio).

In 1984, we began to develop a formative and summative system that could meet faculty, student, administrator, and unit needs. Our first approach used a mainframe database package that allowed us to develop an application that nonprogrammers could use to collect and report on student ratings. By capitalizing on institutional data sources such as the registration system's course file and student file, we were able to search across various sets of data. This allowed us to identify courses and students and to locate and group them in ways that allowed various kinds of analyses. For example, we could examine changes over time, across disciplines, and among class sizes. The great value of this approach is that it combines the power of evaluation with assessment with other institutional data to serve multiple purposes.

This was essential for cost-effective comparison between databases and for automating the production of evaluation materials (questionnaires, packages, and labels), as well as the automated production of reports and maintenance of a suite of ratings questionnaires. Another key design feature of the database strategy was building an item bank in which a master list of items was maintained to support the development of many questionnaire versions. This allowed the use of a core set of items for summative purposes and a wide variety of descriptive items that could provide useful and confidential feedback for teaching improvement purposes. As a result, everyone received two reports: (1) one of the core of ten items required for summative purposes and (2) a confidential report of any other diagnostic items requested by the instructor.

In 1986, we received a grant from the Fund for the Improvement of Postsecondary Education (FIPSE) to continue to develop our system. We worked on (1) developing questionnaires and reporting formats that could serve both formative and summative evaluation purposes; (2) finding effective ways to report ratings results to a various kinds of ratings users (students, faulty, and administrators); and (3) finding cost-effective ways to introduce faculty to the literature of teaching improvement.

By the time the first phase was complete, our database management system was transferred from the mainframe environment to the newly emerging PC environment. We developed and tested the Course Evaluation System (CES) at several universities. We found it to be an effective tool for accurately and flexibly collecting and reporting ratings with a rapid turnaround. CES provided for every aspect of the operation, from preparing questionnaires and packing materials to scanning answer sheets using standard optical mark readers and printing reports of the results. Reports were as clear and unambiguous as possible. We included item mean scores and descriptive statistics, confidence intervals for each course and each instructor using a sample of courses taught by that instructor, and a departmental comparison (similar courses in the same subject area at the same level in similar-sized classes). CES reports also displayed graphic illustrations to reduce over-reliance on mean scores and over-interpretation of small differences between means.

During this time, computing technology made the critical shift from DOS to Microsoft Windows. We were able to handle evaluations from six thousand classes each academic year with only the services of a single evaluation professional and a secretary, supported by occasional agency temps or student employees to manage peak loads of packing and unpacking forms. A shift to a new and even larger institution led to an upgrade of the CES system. This improved on the original design by allowing more powerful data management operations, improving query functions, making finer comparisons for normative purposes, and managing the ever-increasing amount of historical data required for that purpose.

TCE-Tools. In the most recent version, called TCE-Tools, all of the previous features and functions have been retained, but many features were created to meet the everyday needs of the staff who operate the system. In its simplest use, it remains a tool for conducting high-quality service without having advanced technical professionals on staff. But now TCE-Tools has many of the conveniences that such professionals find useful (for example, sophisticated queries, integration of data sets, and extraction of related data from different locations to create tables and reports). Other features include support for individualized questionnaires (for example, "cafeteria style" forms) and delivery of Web-based on-line course evaluations.

Over the nearly two decades since we began, having an increasingly powerful software tool has made it possible for us to capitalize on economy of scale and synergy to provide high-quality ratings services and, at the same time, maintain the essential consultation and development services that allowed us to help ratings users make better use of data. Our reporting formats actually improved the accuracy of users' interpretations of ratings data (Franklin and Theall, forthcoming). Our ability to provide a suite of ratings forms with the same resources that it would take to do a single form gave us much more leeway and more opportunities to work with academic units in creating better, fairer evaluation systems. In short, technology let us spend more time with the people who would use the ratings and, in turn, bring what we learned back to decisions about the way we use the technology. We learned some important lessons along the way:

- Use a systematic approach that establishes the roles and purposes of evaluation, develops strategies to meet specific needs, and considers the entirety of the context and environment.
- Get and use expert assistance on database design and maintenance, data processing, statistical analysis, and report design.
- Create an appropriate organizational infrastructure with skilled staff to operate the system. Administrators often thought that software alone could provide service. Our goal was to show how much more service staff could provide with good data processing tools.
- Establish clear lines of responsibility, reporting, and supervision for those who administer the system. The highly charged nature of evaluating faculty requires organizational independence and stability over time.
- Invest in the evaluation system, keep software tools and computing systems up to date, and regularly train staff as needed for updates in systems technology. Judiciously spending more for a good system or good advice saves a lot of time and money later.
- Evaluate the evaluation system for timeliness, accuracy, efficiency, and effectiveness on a regular basis.

Advantages of Using Technology to Support Evaluation. We have been deliberately cautious about the use of technology to support summative evaluation. However, our concerns do not deny the potential of technology to provide mechanisms for both formative and summative purposes as well as teaching improvement. Here are some examples:

- The simplicity with which technology can be used to gather and store quantitative and qualitative data makes technology use not only advisable but in some cases absolutely necessary. For example, in on-line courses that employ conferencing utilities, archives of student-student and student-teacher dialogue can be kept for review or formal analysis. Paper systems simply cannot provide this depth and quantity of rich data.

- At the same time, the use of technology dramatically reduces the amount of paper used and can simplify the distribution of forms and collection of data. It saves time, money, and paper.
- Processing speed is an obvious benefit, and although this should not be the controlling factor, the value of rapid response to individuals or groups is obvious in most instructional situations.
- Asynchronous communication, not bounded by the physical or chronological constraints of scheduled weekly class meetings, can enhance student-teacher dialogue and provide a resource for formative evaluation. Although there is insufficient research to predict student behaviors in technology-rich environments, anecdotal reports and discussion on professional listservs suggest that using technology even as a supplement to a traditional face-to-face class can open new avenues to dialogue and understanding of course content and, equally important, shared perspectives about the importance and relevance of that content.
- We cannot ignore the potential of technology to support curricular and program evaluation. Consider the benefits to students, teachers, and departments involved in large-enrollment, multisection service courses. Technology can be used to support assessment activities, ongoing formative evaluation, and content review. Equally important in multisection courses, the use of technology for such purposes provides efficient and effective ways to present standardized, coherent, accessible information to all students. Quality control and course management are made easier.

The list of advantages is extensive and limited only by the amount of creative effort put into designing instruction that most effectively incorporates technology. Because truly well-designed instruction includes carefully constructed objectives, thorough assessment, and careful evaluation, the use of technology should not be thought of as an adjunct issue or as a mechanism for evaluation but as part of a complete and systematic approach to teaching and learning.

Conclusions

There is an old saying: "When you have a hammer, everything becomes a nail." In evaluation, the choice and the use of appropriate tools is critical because the evaluation of teaching is a complex and difficult task, made more difficult because of the particular pressures that attend any measurement of performance and assignment of rewards. Sound measurement technique is an absolute requirement, but sound policies and process are equally important. Whatever the systems used for data collection, management, analysis, and reporting, they must serve both the institution and the individuals concerned. We should not let evaluation be framed around the array of available tools. We must first determine the needed functions and then let the form take shape.

References

Arreola, R. A. *Developing a Comprehensive Faculty Evaluation System.* (2nd ed.) Bolton, Mass.: Anker, 2000.

Balasubramanian, N. V. (ed.). *Teaching and Learning Quality Management through Use of Information Technology.* Hong Kong: University Grants Committee, 1999.

Balcombe, A. "Using the Internet as a Medium for Questionnaire Data Collection." In N. V. Balasubramanian (ed.), *Teaching and Learning Quality Management through Use of Information Technology.* Hong Kong: University Grants Committee, 1999.

Chu, G. C., and Schramm, W. *Learning from Television: What the Research Says.* Washington, D.C.: National Society of Professionals in Telecommunications, 1967.

Franklin, J., and Theall, M. "Who Reads Ratings: Knowledge, Attitudes, and Practices of Users of Student Ratings of Instruction." Paper presented at the annual meeting of the American Educational Research Association, San Francisco, Mar. 1989. (ED 306 241)

Franklin, J., and Theall, M. "Communicating Student Ratings Results to Decision Makers: Design for Good Practice." In M. Theall and J. Franklin (eds), *Student Ratings of Instruction: Issues for Improving Practice.* New Directions for Teaching and Learning, no 43. San Francisco: Jossey-Bass, 1990.

Franklin, J., and Theall, M. "Thinking about Faculty Thinking about Teacher and Course Evaluation Results." In N. Hativa and P. Goodyear (eds.), *Teacher Thinking, Beliefs, and Knowledge in Higher Education.* New York: Kluwer, forthcoming.

Green, K. C. "The Continuing Challenge of Instructional Integration and User Support." In *Campus Computing 1999: The Sixth National Survey of Information Technology in Higher Education.* Encino, Calif.: Campus Computing Project, 1999.

Ha, T. S. "Issues and Problems in Implementing and Maintaining a Web-Based SET system." Paper presented at the Southeast Asia Regional Workshop on the Issues and Problems of Using the World Wide Web for Student Evaluation of Teaching in Higher Education Institutions, Hong Kong, Feb. 2001.

Ha, T. S., and Marsh, J. "Implementation of a System for On-Line Evaluation of Teaching." In N. V. Balasubramanian (ed.), *Teaching and Learning Quality Management through Use of Information Technology.* Hong Kong: University Grants Committee, 1999.

Hmieleski, K., and Champagne, M. "Plugging in to Course Evaluation." *Technical Horizons in Education· The Source,* Sept.-Oct. 2000. Available on-line at http://horizon.unc.edu/TS/assessment/2000-09.asp

Lai-kuen, K., and Kamel, N. "Quality Management in Higher Education." In N. V. Balasubramanian (ed.), *Teaching and Learning Quality Management through Use of Information Technology.* Hong Kong: University Grants Committee, 1999a.

Lai-kuen, K., and Kamel, N. "UNINET: Student Teacher Communication." In N. V. Balasubramanian (ed.), *Teaching and Learning Quality Management through Use of Information Technology.* Hong Kong: University Grants Committee, 1999b.

Lo, T., Wong, W., Barrett, J., and Wong, C. *An Evaluation Sourcebook for Higher Education in Hong Kong.* Hong Kong: University Grants Committee, 1999a.

Lo, T., Wong, W., Barrett, J., and Wong, C. "The Design and Development of an On-Line Questionnaire Builder." In N. V. Balasubramanian (ed.), *Teaching and Learning Quality Management through Use of Information Technology.* Hong Kong: University Grants Committee, 1999b.

Mah, P. "Implementation of the Web Teaching Evaluation System at Hong Kong Baptist University." Paper presented at the Southeast Asia Regional Workshop on the Issues and Problems of Using the World Wide Web for Student Evaluation of Teaching in Higher Education Institutions, Hong Kong, Feb. 2001.

Ng, K. W. "WebSET: A System for On-Line Student Evaluation of Teaching." Paper presented at the Southeast Asia Regional Workshop on the Issues and Problems of Using the World Wide Web for Student Evaluation of Teaching in Higher Education Institutions, Hong Kong, Feb. 2001.

Olubbemiro, J. J. Keynote Address at the Southeast Asia Regional Workshop on the Issues and Problems of Using the World Wide Web for Student Evaluation of Teaching in Higher Education Institutions, Hong Kong, Feb. 2001.

Russell, T. L. *The No Significant Difference Phenomenon.* Raleigh, N.C.: North Carolina State University Office of Instructional Telecommunications, 1999.

Shah, A., and Lo, T. "Going On-Line with Student Evaluation of Teaching." Paper presented at the Southeast Asia Regional Workshop on the Issues and Problems of Using the World Wide Web for Student Evaluation of Teaching in Higher Education Institutions, Hong Kong, Feb. 2001.

Theall, M. "Electronic Course Evaluation Is Not Necessarily the Answer." *Technical Horizons in Education: The Source.* Nov.-Dec., 2000. Available on-line at http://horizon .unc.edu/TS/letters/2000–11.asp

Theall, M., and Franklin, J. (eds.). *Student Ratings of Instruction: Issues for Improving Practice.* New Directions for Teaching and Learning, no. 43. San Francisco: Jossey-Bass, 1990a.

Theall, M , and Franklin, J. "Student Ratings in the Context of Complex Evaluation Systems." In M. Theall and J. Franklin, (eds.), *Student Ratings of Instruction: Issues for Improving Practice.* New Directions for Teaching and Learning, no. 43. San Francisco: Jossey-Bass, 1990b.

Theall, M., and Franklin, J. (eds.). *Effective Practices for Improving Teaching.* New Directions for Teaching and Learning, no. 48. San Francisco: Jossey-Bass, 1991a.

Theall, M., and Franklin, J. "Using Student Ratings for Teaching Improvement." In M. Theall and J. Franklin (eds.), *Effective Practices for Improving Teaching.* New Directions for Teaching and Learning, no. 48. San Francisco: Jossey-Bass, 1991b.

MICHAEL THEALL *is associate professor of educational leadership and director of the Center for Teaching and Learning at the University of Illinois, Springfield.*

JENNIFER FRANKLIN *is director of the Center for Teaching and Learning and the California State University at Dominguez Hills.*

Formative evaluation is at the heart of any effort to improve teaching, scholarly teaching, and the scholarship of teaching and learning. Methods are presented that can improve practice in each of these areas and support a transformation in the way we think about the work of teaching.

Formative Evaluation and the Scholarship of Teaching and Learning

Ronald Smith

We are in the midst of a major change in the way we think about teaching and about the nature of faculty work. Becoming more scholarly (or professional) about teaching has led to the idea of scholarly teaching and a scholarship of teaching and learning. This transformation in how faculty members view their work as teachers will require learning and change that needs to be informed and supported by formative feedback. Formative feedback or evaluation is at the heart of any effort to improve practice. In this chapter, I examine a repertoire of methods available to provide formative feedback to help to improve teaching, scholarly teaching, and the scholarship of teaching and learning.

Scriven (1991) describes evaluation as "the process, whose duty is the systematic and objective determination of merit, worth, or value. Without such a process, there is no way to distinguish the worthwhile from the worthless" (p. 4). In practice, evaluation is often not as systematic or objective as Scriven suggests.

A summative evaluation is a somewhat final decision about merit, worth, or value. Is this student's work good enough to be graded "pass"? Is this teacher's teaching, research, or service good enough to merit contract renewal? Is this research paper good enough to be published? In all cases, there are criteria and standards, either explicit or implicit, to assess merit, worth, or value—to determine what is "good enough." I am not suggesting that *just* good enough is an adequate standard, rather that performance needs to meet *some* standard. Much has already been written about the summative evaluation of teaching. This chapter focuses on formative evaluation.

The distinction between formative and summative evaluation is not self-evident. For example, one might argue that the summative evaluation of teaching in personnel decisions is designed to improve the quality of teaching in the institution. Here I use the term *formative evaluation* (or feedback) to refer to the actions and activities initiated *by the individual* teacher, with the intent to collect information to inform *decisions about how to improve.* This reflects a frame of mind and an approach to professional practice that has, at its core, the desire to be effective, to monitor current performance against some standard by collecting information, and to make decisions both about the effectiveness of current practice and about how to improve.

Teaching, Scholarly Teaching, and the Scholarship of Teaching and Learning

Teaching refers to designing and implementing activities to promote student learning. Teaching goes beyond what a teacher does in the classroom and depends largely on course design, the development of instructional materials, and the out-of-class interactions between faculty members and students, as well as the formative and summative assessment of student learning. Barr and Tagg (1995) suggest that a new paradigm for institutions should be "to produce learning" rather than "to provide instruction" (p. 13). Biggs (1999) argues that we must focus on what the student does if we are to teach for quality learning.

All faculty members have the obligation to teach well. Good teaching engages students and fosters significant long-lasting learning. Good teaching is clearly necessary, worthwhile, and valuable in its own right. Although learning can occur without the benefit of teaching, teaching has no purpose other than to enable learning. Improving teaching requires faculty learning. That learning will rarely occur without feedback.

Scholarly Teaching. All teachers should be knowledgeable about their subject matter. It is unfortunate, however, that being a scholar in your field has often been the only condition for employability as a university teacher. Scholarly teaching demands more. Scholarly teachers apply educational theory and research to their own practice (Weimer, Menges, and Associates, 1996). Scholarly teaching requires that teachers and their teaching be informed, not only by the latest ideas in their field but by existing theory, research, and practical ideas about student learning and teaching in their field, instructional design, teaching and learning styles, and methods of assessment. Scholarly teachers are aware of teaching alternatives and able to choose appropriately for the students in their classes.

Brookfield (1990, 1995) reflects the difference between teaching and scholarly teaching by distinguishing the skillful teacher from the critically reflective teacher. He suggests that the former is concerned "primarily with the nuts and bolts of classroom processes" and that we need to go beyond that to become critically reflective and to "identify and scrutinize the assumptions that undergird how we work" (1995, p. xii). The learning required in moving from teaching to being more scholarly about teaching is certainly transformative for most faculty members. It also requires and benefits from formative feedback.

The Scholarship of Teaching and Learning. The scholarship of teaching and learning, as articulated by the Carnegie Academy for the Scholarship of Teaching and Learning (CASTL), "will entail *a public account* of some or all of the full act of teaching—vision, design, enactment, outcomes, and analysis—in a manner susceptible to *critical review* by the teacher's professional peers and *amenable to productive employment* in future work by members of the same community" (Shulman, 1998, p. 6, emphasis added).

I distinguish *teaching* (activities to promote student learning) from *scholarly teaching* (a reflection of one's knowledge about and approach to teaching and learning) and the *scholarship of teaching and learning* (the contributions to a developing body of knowledge about teaching and learning). It is a significant transformation to change one's view of teaching from an activity that derives from scholarly work in the discipline to one that can and should be informed by the substantial and growing body of knowledge about teaching and learning in higher education. The scholarship of teaching and learning and the idea that any faculty member, not just those in education, could and possibly even should contribute to it, extends this transformation of the nature of the roles and responsibilities of faculty members as teachers. As detailed in Figure 6.1, formative evaluation can contribute to improving

Figure 6.1. Formative Evaluation and Improved Practice

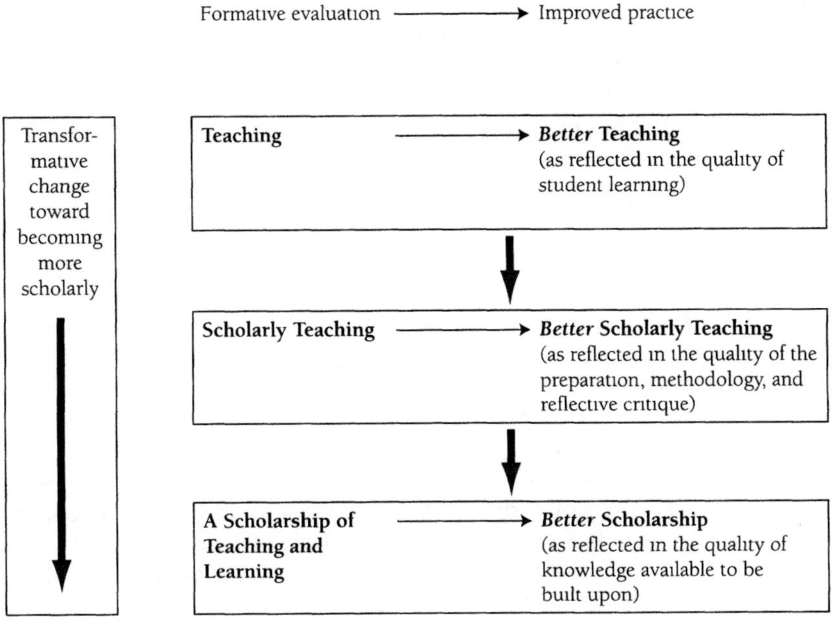

Formative evaluation ————▶ Improved practice

Transfor-mative change toward becoming more scholarly	Teaching ————▶ **Better Teaching** (as reflected in the quality of student learning)
	⬇
	Scholarly Teaching ————▶ **Better Scholarly Teaching** (as reflected in the quality of the preparation, methodology, and reflective critique)
	⬇
	A Scholarship of Teaching and Learning ————▶ **Better Scholarship** (as reflected in the quality of knowledge available to be built upon)

practice in each of these areas, as well as to stimulating and supporting the transformation in how we think about the work of teaching.

Formative Evaluation and Improving Teaching

The formative evaluation of teaching can be described in terms of the source of the information (self, students, peers, and experts), as well as the method used to collect the information (questionnaires, observations, interviews) and the degree of time, effort, and formality involved. Teaching can also be improved without any particular awareness of, or reference to, any specific formal knowledge about learning or teaching. The conscientious teacher can improve his or her teaching and can increase student learning without moving very far in the direction of becoming a more scholarly teacher.

There are incidental or informal ways that teachers get information that can lead to improvements in their teaching and in their students' learning. Teachers often mention reading their students' body language or overhearing student comments; others note the quality of student work on assignments; some claim to be intuitive and "just know" how it is going. Schön (1983) talks about those professionals who "deliberately involve themselves in the messy but crucially important problems [of teaching] and, when asked to describe their methods of inquiry, they speak of experience, trial and error, intuition, and muddling through" (p. 42). It would require further investigation to determine to what extent these actions actually lead to improvements in student learning. It would require a more scholarly approach.

There are also more formal and deliberate methods for collecting information to inform decision making in support of improving teaching and learning, that is, formative evaluation. Let's first look at methods that usually involve only students and then those that involve colleagues.

Input from Students. The following writers provide a wide range of ideas for obtaining student feedback about teaching.

- Angelo and Cross (1983) wrote *Classroom Assessment Techniques: A Handbook for College Teachers* "as a practical how-to-do-it book that college teachers can use to assess the quality of teaching and learning in their own classrooms" (p. xiv). Fifty different classroom assessment techniques (CATs) are presented. They can be used for assessing course-related knowledge and skills, for assessing learner attitudes, values, and self-awareness, and for assessing learner reactions to instruction.
- *Tools for Teaching* (Davis, 1993) has a chapter devoted to "fast feedback techniques" that "require modest effort, are easy to carry out, and use little class time" (p. 345). These methods include distributing blank index cards at the end of class with such questions as "What do you want more of? Less of?" (pp. 346–349).

- McBride, Ruttan, and Rice (the Web; n.d.) provide formative evaluation instruments for designing Web-based instruction. Steve Ehrmann and the Flashlight Group have designed the *Current Student Inventory* as an evaluation toolkit for the formative evaluation of either teaching strategies or students' use of technologies (http://tltgroup.org).
- Leiberman (1999) provides examples of how CATs can be implemented using technology, called Techno-CATs.
- *How Am I Teaching? Forms and Activities for Acquiring Instructional Input* (Weimer, Parrett, and Kerns, 1988) provides a catalogue of twelve methods for collecting information from students, colleagues, or yourself about the impact of current instructional strategies during a course. Each comes with suggestions for when and how it should be used.

Input from Colleagues. A number of techniques have been described for getting input from colleagues to enhance teaching.

- The term *peer-partner programs* describes a family of teaching-improvement strategies called alliances for change (Tiberius, Sackin, Janzen, and Preece, 1993) or partners in learning (Katz and Henry, 1988) that involve colleagues in working with each other in a systematic way in a well-structured program (Morrison, 1997). These programs usually have pairs of faculty members working together for at least a semester in a helping relationship that includes visiting each other's classes, talking with students, and meeting regularly to discuss their teaching and how it can be improved.
- *Small group instructional diagnosis* (SGID) (Clark and Bekey, 1979; Lenze, 1997) is a technique for collecting data from students about their reactions to teaching. It requires twenty to thirty minutes of class time under the direction of someone (a colleague or a staff developer) trained in using this method. Leiberman (1999, p. 145) describes an electronic SGID.
- *Instructional Skills Program* (ISW) is a laboratory approach to the improvement of learning and teaching (Morrison, 1985). It is an intensive four-day workshop for four to six participants conducted by teachers for teachers. Participants review basic ideas about teaching, check current practices, and, within the safe environment of the workshop, try new strategies and techniques, all with a view to improving their teaching.
- Teachers can use other methods. Examples include reviewing students' notes, watching videos of their teaching, or preparing a teaching portfolio. There are excellent resources (Brinko and Menges, 1997; Knapper and Piccinin, 1999) that provide examples and details on how staff developers working as consultants can help faculty improve their teaching.

The methods just described help teachers become more effective by collecting data on what is working and what is not and then working out ways to improve, either on their own or with the help of colleagues. Although it is often a challenge to decide exactly what should be done with what is discovered, these activities are still very important. They reflect one aspect of what it means to be more professional about teaching—to be actively engaged in monitoring the impact of one's work and committed to improving one's effectiveness.

Many of these methods are probably familiar to most faculty members, even if they are not so common in practice. The methods themselves contain and reflect the results of research on teaching and learning—for example, the dimensions of effective instruction and specific teaching behaviors that correlate with overall teaching effectiveness. Even so, their use may not transformative.

Argyris and Schön (1974) talk of individuals as always striving to be effective, that is, to achieve their intentions. Learning is the detection and correction of the gaps between what we intend to produce and what actually happens. Feedback is essential to this learning. "Single-loop learning" is coming to use more effective action strategies to reach their goals, without changing the basic assumptions or values. An example is becoming a more effective lecturer without questioning the value of lectures. "Double-loop learning" involves changing the very criteria or values by which effectiveness is judged. For example, a good teacher must be a scholarly teacher; improving teaching means improving learning rather than improving lecturing.

The movement toward scholarly teaching raises the bar beyond just being conscientious enough to collect information in order to improve. It suggests that in order to become more professional (and more effective), teachers need to become more knowledgeable (scholarly) about teaching and learning (Smith, 1997). The methods in the next section can do more than just help teachers become more scholarly; they can also help with double-loop learning and transform teachers' view of the nature of their work.

Formative Evaluation and Scholarly Teaching

The methods in this section are designed to improve the explicit attention to and awareness of the body of knowledge that exists about teaching and learning in higher education. Although many of the methods for gathering information are similar to those in the previous section, the context within which they are used is not. In general, the methods are ways to learn more about teaching and learning and to assess the impact of using that knowledge to inform practice. Such learning will necessarily involve some form of feedback from self, students, colleagues, or experts (see Table 6.1), although it is difficult to separate out the sources, as was done in the previous section.

Dialogue. Reading and discussing provide means for faculty to acquire new knowledge and to develop and refine their understanding through dialogue within their community of practice. Some people might not think of these activities as formative or as providing feedback. But if we read with a view to testing our current ideas and ways of thinking against an author's or if we talk with colleagues with a view to testing our ideas, then we are

Table 6.1. Formative Evaluation Methods and Teaching Scholarship

	Self	Students	Colleagues	Experts
Teaching	Incidental, informal, intuitive, trial-and-error	CATs, fast feedback, current student inventory	SGID, ISW, peer partners	Teaching consultants
Scholarly Teaching	Reading and discussion groups; book clubs Action research and classroom research Critical reflection Listservs			
Scholarship of Teaching and Learning	Peer collaboration and peer review Course portfolio Carnegie Scholars Program Journal and grant reviewers On-line journals and discussion groups			

certainly collecting information; we are acquiring knowledge that can inform our practice. However, becoming a better scholarly teacher involves not only coming to know more about the literature on teaching and learning, as important as that is. It also involves reflective technique.

Critical Reflection. Brookfield (1995) offers specific suggestions for how we might *critically reflect* on (and improve) our practice by using "four distinct, though interconnecting lenses . . . autobiographical reflection . . . our students' eyes . . . our colleagues' perceptions and experiences . . . and literature" (p. viii). Critical reflection helps us take informed actions and develop a rationale for practice, which are all characteristics of scholarly work (Glassick, Huber, and Maeroff, 1997). Reflection involves assessment of *what is* in relation to *what might or should be* and includes feedback designed to reduce the gap. In other words, it can support single- or double-loop learning.

Kreber and Cranton (2000) contend that when faculty members "engage in reflection on content, process, and premise in the domains of instructional, pedagogical, and curricular knowledge, through classroom or action research, this should count as scholarly activity" (p. 492). They offer suggestions for how we might construct knowledge in each of the domains through reflection, for example, through holding discussions, reading, keeping a log, writing, collecting feedback, and conducting action research. They describe these activities as serving "a formative purpose because they facilitate the assessment of faculty's learning about teaching either through self-evaluation or interactions with a faculty developer" (pp. 488–489). All learning, including self-directed learning, requires formative feedback.

Formative feedback is necessary, not only on the effectiveness of our actions but on the adequacy of our understanding. Action research and classroom research are examples of systematic inquiry into teaching and learning situations. Cross and Steadman (1996) show how classroom assessment techniques can go beyond merely assessing the impact of one's teaching on one's student. "Classroom Assessment describes what *is* happening; Classroom Research tries to find out *why*" (p. 7). Moving beyond describing *what* students are learning from a particular assignment or activity to examining *why* some methods work better for particular students is part of what it means to be *scholarly* about one's teaching. Another part of being scholarly involves implementing alternative strategies and monitoring their effectiveness.

The case studies in their book (Cross and Steadman, 1996) provide examples of how teachers can use various classroom assessment techniques as part of a more systematic and ongoing inquiry into particular issues of teaching and learning in the context of their own classrooms. These investigations recognize and build on the work of others. The result is that "teachers are learning how to become more effective teachers, and students are learning how to become more effective learners" (p. 2).

These case studies are examples of scholarly teaching. To the extent that the results of these inquiries are made public and available for use by others, they can contribute to a scholarship of teaching and learning. In the next section, I present some examples of how formative evaluation is necessary to the development of the concept, as well as the methods and techniques of a scholarship of teaching and learning.

Formative Evaluation and a Scholarship of Teaching and Learning

A scholarship of teaching and learning "requires a kind of 'going meta' in which faculty frame and systematically investigate questions related to student learning—the conditions under which it occurs, what it looks like, how to deepen it, and so forth—*and* to do so with an eye not only to improving their own classroom but *to advancing practice beyond it*" (Hutchings and Shulman, 1999, p. 13, emphasis added). Cambridge (2000) argues that in order to be seen as scholarly work *and* to contribute to knowledge and advance practice, faculty need "to go public with their findings, to receive the kind of peer review that interrogates their methods and conclusions, and to change their teaching and their scholarly investigations of teaching based on that review" (p. 56).

Most faculty members have had no explicit or formal training in the scholarship of teaching and learning. They bring to the activity their training as scholars in their disciplines, but they are novices as *scholars of teaching*. They need *to develop* and *to learn how to develop* the expertise needed to contribute to a scholarship of teaching (Smith, 2001). This is different from a chemist learning to do history, in the sense that history is already well defined as a field of study with well-developed and commonly accepted methodologies. The development of a scholarship of teaching and learning is still in its very early stages, so the participants are, in fact, engaged in constructing both the knowledge and the methods that will define the field of practice. What types of evaluative feedback will help form this new field of inquiry and practice?

As with every field of study, formative evaluation can be used to improve both the content (the body of knowledge created) and the process (the methods used to create that knowledge). Formative feedback, usually from colleagues, is a key feature of the examples that follow. Colleagues, working together, invite, offer, and receive information about the quality of what they are doing (the individual inquiry project), with a view to improving its quality. In the ideal case, there is also information about how things are being done (the types and format of their interactions) that can lead to improvements in the methods as well as the outcomes.

Peer Collaboration and Peer Review. Hutchings (1996) provides a menu, with examples, of how feedback through collaborative work can help identify and improve the methods for creating a scholarship of teaching and learning. These include using teaching circles, making reciprocal classroom visits and observations, mentoring and coaching, and teaching teams, as well as using collaborative inquiry and departmental occasions for collaboration, which include hiring and intercampus collaboration and external peer review.

- The Course Portfolio is one example of how the ongoing conversations within the AAHE Course Portfolio Working Group led individuals to improve their inquiries into their own teaching and how they made it public. Another part of being scholarly is figuring out "how to generate exchange, and build on knowledge in order to improve practice" (Hutchings, 1998, p. 1). Martsolf (1998) describes how the process of creating the portfolio leads to a focus on student learning: "Weekly student reflections, solicited in order to fill out the portfolio with relevant evidence, helped me to clarify, and therefore more immediately address and correct, student misconceptions" (p. 28). The feedback not only led to improved inquiry and documentation; it also led to improved learning. Cerbin (1996) reports how he came to think of a course as scholarly project and "now see[s] that the course portfolio is like a scholarly manuscript—not a finished publication, but a manuscript, a draft of an ongoing inquiry" (pp. 52–53). Both the form and the content of the portfolio benefited from feedback from colleagues.

- The Carnegie Scholars Program is an example of how faculty members are being encouraged and supported to work together in a formative way "to craft a set of projects that will 'add up' and build upon one another," with a "commitment to documenting and sharing results . . . [which] may well entail the invention of new forms, genres, vehicles, and media for preserving and presenting what is learned" (Carnegie, 1999, p. 4). This development of a scholarship of teaching and learning includes formative feedback and takes place within a supportive community of scholars.

They are working together to invent, develop, and refine the methods for making teaching public, to determine what is appropriate and helpful critique, and to explore how the knowledge can be used and built upon.

Reviews for Grant Programs and Journals. Teaching development grant programs provide opportunities for faculty to not only to engage in teaching scholarship but to receive formative feedback on how to improve their projects, both the successful and unsuccessful ones. We still need to invent more effective means of sharing the results of this work with colleagues.

Faculty who submit an article to one of the many journals now available on teaching in general (for example, the *Journal of Excellence in College Teaching*) or to more than fifty disciplinary teaching journals (Weimer, 1993) receive formative, as well as summative, feedback on their work. Reviews of proposals submitted to teaching conferences provide feedback that serves to enhance teaching scholarship. Examining what type of feedback is most helpful to faculty in improving the quality of their work—that is, collecting feedback of the effectiveness of the feedback—is an area that requires investigation. It is an example of how formative feedback could improve an important process.

The Journal of Scholarship of Teaching and Learning is a new Web-based, peer-reviewed journal (Isaacson, 2000) that grew out of "an interest in creating a forum that would encourage faculty to share their knowledge and inquiry into the teaching-learning process" (p. 3). The articles in the first issues deal with specific inquiries into issues in teaching, active learning in accounting, teaching critical thinking, project-based instruction, as well as with questions about why we should have a scholarship of teaching and learning (Shulman, 2000). The journal offers on-line access to the articles, as well as threaded discussions about them, providing formative input into both the content and the methods of further inquiries.

Conclusions

I have argued that formative evaluation is essential to the learning necessary for faculty to improve teaching, scholarly teaching, and a scholarship of teaching. I have distinguished these three activities and offered examples of formative feedback that can help each of them improve in their own right. The methods are most well developed for improving teaching and are in the process of being created for a scholarship of teaching and learning.

There is a substantial body of research on the summative evaluation of teaching, but much less is known about the various formative feedback methods. We need to know more about when and how to use the various methods; we need to monitor the effectiveness of the strategies we use; and we need to assess their impact and be critically reflective about this area of our practice. We need to know much more about how to use the information that is collected from students and colleagues. If this information is made public, it can also contribute to a scholarship of teaching and learning. In short, we need to become more scholarly about formative evaluation.

Teaching can not only be improved in its own right through formative feedback but teachers may improve their teaching by becoming more scholarly and contributing to a scholarship of teaching and learning. Formative evaluation in the form of collegial interaction and support is also necessary to promote and sustain the learning required for this transformation in the way faculty members think about the practice and profession of teaching in higher education and about their work as teachers.

References

Angelo, T. A., and Cross, K. P. *Classroom Assessment Techniques: A Handbook for College Teachers.* (2nd ed.) San Francisco: Jossey-Bass, 1993.

Argyris, C., and Schon, D. A. *Theory in Practice: Increasing Professional Effectiveness.* San Francisco: Jossey-Bass, 1974.

Barr, R. B., and Tagg, J. "From Teaching to Learning: A New Paradigm for Undergraduate Education." *Change,* Nov./Dec. 1995, 27, 13–25.

Biggs, J. B. *Teaching for Quality Learning at University: What the Student Does.* SRHE and Open University Press: Buckingham, England, 1999.

Boyer, E. *Scholarship Reconsidered: Priorities of the Professoriate.* Princeton, N.J.: Princeton University Press, 1990.

Brinko, K. T., and Menges, R. J. (eds.). *Practically Speaking: A Sourcebook for Instructional Consultants in Higher Education.* Stillwater, Okla.: New Forums Press, 1997.

Brookfield, S. D. *The Skillful Teacher: On Technique, Trust, and Responsiveness in the Classroom.* San Francisco: Jossey-Bass, 1990.

Brookfield, S. D. *Becoming a Critically Reflective Teacher.* San Francisco: Jossey-Bass, 1995.

Cambridge, B. L. "The Scholarship of Teaching and Learning: A National Initiative." In M. Kaplan and D. Leiberman (eds.), *To Improve the Academy,* 2000, 18, 55–68.

Carnegie Foundation for the Advancement of Teaching. *Information and Applications for the Pew National Fellowship Program for Carnegie Scholars: The Teaching Academy Campus Program; Work with the Scholarly and Professional Societies.* Menlo Park, Calif.: Carnegie Foundation, 1999.

Cerbin, W. "Inventing a New Genre: The Course Portfolio at the University of Wisconsin-La Crosse." In P. Hutchings (ed.), *Making Teaching Community Property: A Menu for Peer Collaboration and Peer Review.* Washington, D.C.: American Association for Higher Education, 1996.

Clark, D. J., and Bekey, J. "Use of Small Groups in Instructional Evaluation." *Professional and Organizational Development Quarterly,* 1979, 1, 87–95.

Cross, K. P., and Steadman, M. H. *Classroom Research: Implementing the Scholarship of Teaching.* San Francisco. Jossey-Bass, 1996.

Davis, B. G. *Tools for Teaching.* San Francisco. Jossey-Bass. 1993.

Glassick, C. E., Huber, M. T., and Maeroff, G. I. *Scholarship Assessed: Evaluation of the Professoriate.* San Francisco: Jossey-Bass, 1997.

Hutchings, P. (ed.). *Making Teaching Community Property: A Menu for Peer Collaboration and Peer Review.* Washington, D.C.: American Association for Higher Education, 1996.

Hutchings, P. (ed.). *The Course Portfolio: How Faculty Can Examine Their Teaching to Advance Practice and Improve Student Learning.* Washington, D.C.: American Association for Higher Education, 1998.

Hutchings, P., and Shulman, L. S. "The Scholarship of Teaching: New Elaborations, New Developments. *Change,* 1999, 31(5), 11–15.

Isaacson, R. "Why JoSoTL and Why Now?" *The Journal of Scholarship of Teaching and Learning*, 2000, *1*(1). http://www.iusb.edu/~josotl/Vol1No1/isaacson.pdf

Katz J., and Henry, M. *Turning Professors into Teachers: A New Approach to Faculty Development and Student Learning.* New York: ACE/Macmillan, 1988.

Knapper C., and Piccinin, S. (eds.). *Using Consultants to Improve Practice.* New Directions for Teaching and Learning, no. 79. San Francisco: Jossey-Bass, 1999.

Kreber, C., and Cranton, P. "Exploring the Scholarship of Teaching." *Journal of Higher Education*, 2000, *71*(4), 476–495.

Leiberman, D. A. "Evaluating Teaching through Electronic Classroom Assessment." In P. Seldin and Associates, *Changing Practice in Evaluating Teaching: A Practical Guide to Improved Faculty Performance and Promotion/Tenure Decisions.* San Francisco: Jossey-Bass, 1999.

Lenze, L. F. "Small Group Instructional Diagnosis (SGID)." In K. Brinko and R. Menges (eds), *Practically Speaking: A Sourcebook for Instructional Consultants in Higher Education.* Stillwater, Okla.: New Forums Press, 1997.

Martsolf, D. "A Course Portfolio for a Graduate Nursing Course." In Hutchings, P. (ed.), *The Course Portfolio: How Faculty Can Examine Their Teaching to Advance Practice and Improve Student Learning.* Washington, D.C.: American Association for Higher Education, 1998.

McBride, R. H., Ruttan, J. P., and Rice, J. C. "Formative Evaluation Instruments for Designing Web-based Instruction." http://www.byu.edu/ipt/workshops/evalwbi /form_eval.html

Morrison, D. E. "The Instructional Skills Workshop: An Inter-institutional Approach." *To Improve the Academy*, 1985, *4*, 75–83.

Morrison, D. E. "Overview of Instructional Consultation in North America." In K. Brinko and R. Menges (eds.), *Practically Speaking: A Sourcebook for Instructional Consultants in Higher Education.* Stillwater, Okla.: New Forums Press, 1997.

Schon, D. A *The Reflective Practitioner: How Professionals Think in Action.* New York: Basic Books, 1983.

Scriven, M. *Evaluation Thesaurus.* (4th ed.) Thousand Oaks, Calif.: Sage, 1991.

Shulman, L. S. "Course Anatomy: The Dissection and Analysis of Knowledge through Teaching." In P. Hutchings (ed.), *The Course Portfolio: How Faculty Can Examine Their Teaching to Advance Practice and Improve Student Learning.* Washington, D.C.: American Association for Higher Education, 1998.

Shulman, L. S. "From Minsk To Pinsk: Why a Scholarship of Teaching and Learning?" *The Journal of Scholarship of Teaching and Learning*, 2000, *1*(1). http://www.iusb.edu /~josotl/Vol1No1/shulman.pdf

Smith, R. A. "Making Teaching Count in Canadian Higher Education: Developing a National Agenda." *Teaching and Learning in Higher Education*, 1997, *21*, 1–10.

Smith, R. A. "Expertise and the Scholarship of Teaching." In C. Kreber (ed.), *Scholarship Revisited.* New Directions for Teaching and Learning, no. 86. San Francisco: Jossey-Bass, 2001.

Tiberius, R. G., Sackin, H. D., Janzen, K. R., and Preece, M. "Alliance for Change: A Procedure for Improving Teaching through Conversations with Learners and Partnerships with Colleagues." *Journal of Staff, Program, and Organizational Development*, 1993, *11*(1), 11–23.

Weimer, M. "The Disciplinary Journals on Pedagogy." *Change*, 1993, *25*, 44–51.

Weimer, M , Menges, R. J., and Associates. (eds.). *Teaching on Solid Ground: Using Scholarship to Improve Practice.* San Francisco: Jossey-Bass, 1996.

Weimer, M., Parrett, J. L., and Kerns, M. *How Am I Teaching? Forms and Activities for Acquiring Instructional Input.* Madison, Wisc.: Magna Publications, 1988.

RONALD A. SMITH *is director of the Centre for the Enhancement of Learning and Teaching at the City University of Hong Kong.*

7

Student outcomes, if assessed carefully and used cautiously, may be helpful in evaluating teachers. However, multiple approaches to understanding student outcomes should be linked to overall program evaluation, combined with strong involvement from teachers, and related to ongoing faculty development.

Using Student Outcomes to Evaluate Teaching: A Cautious Exploration

Tara J. Fenwick

There is no doubt that the language of outcomes and competency has dominant currency in business and industry and increasingly in public sector organizations and educational institutions. Accountability is a common rallying cry of stakeholders demanding transparency and quality measured by outcomes. In higher education, a growing movement to harness learning to industrial purposes and economic imperatives has been linked to questions about instructional performance. In fact, a general movement toward assessment in higher education throughout North America, the United Kingdom, and Australia has tried to demonstrate the "value-added" benefit of instruction in higher education. According to Ewell (1995), this movement is evident in curriculum restructuring to achieve higher levels of instructor productivity, a focus on continuous quality improvement, and pressure for instructor and institutional accountability for key performance indicators.

Student learning is one outcome, if not a priority, of higher education in general and teaching in particular. But can student outcomes be used in valid and responsible ways to evaluate and improve teaching within today's complex academic environments? If so, how can student outcomes be configured in relation to teaching without dangerously narrowing and decontextualizing the analysis or scapegoating instructors for students' achievement?

This chapter examines student outcomes as one dimension of a multifaceted program of faculty evaluation. Approaches are suggested for the micro-level and macro-level evaluation of student outcomes. But first, it is critical to examine the contexts affecting student outcomes and the problems in assessing them reliably.

NEW DIRECTIONS FOR TEACHING AND LEARNING, no 88, Winter 2001 © John Wiley & Sons, Inc

63

Critical Considerations in Determining Student Outcomes

Many critical questions about the outcome evaluation in the dynamic ambiguity of pedagogical contexts require address. First, the meanings and perspectives driving the teaching-learning process must be negotiated. What is understood to be *learning* in different contexts, and what indicators of its existence are accepted as trustworthy? What criteria for *good teaching* will govern the examination of student outcomes? Who gets to determine what counts as desirable outcomes for student performance? Instructors in particular disciplines should have maximum involvement in developing these standards and their indicators to suit the teaching in their own disciplines.

Second, the perspectives governing the data collection process must be debated and clarified. What orientation to inquiry will inform the selection and analysis of student outcomes? An interpretive approach argues that faculty and students' meanings and experiences are as important as external evaluators' constructions, and that the learning process is as important as the product (Sergiovanni and Starratt, 2002). Critical or micropolitical perspectives would examine the power relations configuring the teaching and evaluating processes that resulted in particular student outcomes and would question the diverse interests of evaluation (Giroux and McLaren, 1994). A feminist orientation asks how gender, class, and race configure teaching-learning and whose achievements might be invisible according to dominant ideas of what counts as teaching effectiveness and learning outcomes. A psychoanalytic orientation (Britzman, 1998) might question any assessment that does not examine central unconscious psychic struggles and resistances to knowledge of both students and instructors. The point here is to illustrate the complexity of naming and adjudicating student outcomes. No stakeholder in this process can assume that all involved share the same meanings about good teaching, "successful" learning, and valid outcomes. Nor is there a shared universal perspective on these complex issues.

Third, student outcomes are extraordinarily difficult to correlate with specific interventions. Many factors influence learning, and each teaching situation is unique. Outcome studies generally have no control group for comparison purposes, and too many outcomes measures are not tested for reliability, sensitivity to change, and validity in the face of multiple influences.

There are at least three major influences other than teaching on student success: institutional, dispositional, and social. Ramsden and Entwistle (1981) are among those who have studied how the very climate of a department or institution influences changes in student learning by enhancing engagement or disaffection, and by the affordance of modeling, mentoring, mental challenge, and leadership opportunities in daily activities. Other institutional factors that may affect student achievement include class size, adequacy of the facility, availability of learning resources, faculty workload, and overall program effectiveness. Ewell (1995) also argues that institutional student services (such as remedial instructional service), as well as students' changing enrollment status and institution location, have an impact on student outcomes.

Large empirical studies have shown that students' choice of college affects their outcomes. Astin (1978) compared five data sources, including longitudinal studies, to examine the permanence of college effects on student attitudes, beliefs and self-concept, behavioral patterns, and knowledge-competencies in areas ranging from leadership and academic achievement to sports. Although he notes the influences of individual student maturation, gender, ability, and general environment, Astin concludes that college size, climate, and residential experience significantly affect student changes and career development.

Dispositional factors affecting student learning include students' attitude to instruction, as well as individual capability, developmental stage, and willingness to accept responsibility for learning. Social-economic factors include the student's financial situation, prior knowledge and experience, and cultural values. Meanwhile, students are part of the social "community of practice" (Wenger, 1998) of a classroom, department, or institution. Their learning is embedded in their participation in the activities, relationships, and dialogues of this community. Studies in situative learning (Brown and Duguid, 1996; Kirschner and Witson, 1997) have established that no one factor among the complexly entwined dynamics of a learning community can be isolated and measured for its causal impact on individuals' learning.

Finally, time is a critical dimension in learning. What outcomes may be observable during the classes? How might these be different from what can be measured at the end of the instructional period? The most significant outcomes may not be observable in the four-month teaching semester. What new outcomes related to a student's experiences in that class may emerge one or ten years later? Evaluators must account for the temporal trajectory of learning, as well as the other influences on student achievement listed here, for valid assessment of student outcomes.

Today's Changing Contexts Affecting Student Outcomes

Although the correlation of learning outcomes with instructional delivery and environments has long been of concern (Astin, 1978; Banta, 1988; Ramsden and Entwistle, 1981), the conditions of higher education have changed dramatically in the past ten years. Both student outcomes and teaching must be viewed within these broader contextual changes. Ewell (1995) shows that most North American higher education institutions enrolled far more students in the late 1990s than in previous decades, often without a corresponding increase in numbers of instructors. Demographics have shifted markedly: more students are female, part-time, and twenty-five and older. Many require academic remediation. Few fit the traditional model of single-institution, four-year attendance. Many attend multiple institutions and shift programs repeatedly while enrolled, which affects the accurate tracking of student outcomes. New modes of instruction, including on-line delivery and work-based learning programs, also affect teaching and learning performance.

Meanwhile, student achievement cannot help but be affected by what some say is an institutional trend to undervalue teaching while increasing the disciplinary surveillance of faculty through focus on student outcomes. Trowler (1998) argues that these dynamics are causing faculty stress and the use of coping strategies that often compromise teaching. Karpiak (1996) reports that a general undervaluing of teaching in some institutions has led some faculty to anxiety, cynicism, and loss of interest. And as Kember and Gow (1994) have clearly demonstrated, faculty orientations to teaching significantly affect student outcomes.

Approaches to Assessing Student Outcomes

Student outcomes include everything from observable performance and products to invisible processes of change within college and after college. They involve interrelated dimensions of student development: *cognitive, affective, behavioral,* and *psychological.* We should also add *social,* which, following situated learning theorists (Lave and Wenger, 1991), would include students' ability to participate in particular social contexts.

There are wide-ranging approaches to assessing student outcomes. Each has advantages and disadvantages (Fenwick and Parsons, 2000) and yields only partial insight into student learning and instructor effectiveness. Many measures may be meaningless unless related directly to teacher and student purposes. And no single measure is a valid indicator of student outcomes; good assessment uses multiple methods. However, outcome assessment can yield valuable information that can be used to address learners' problems and enhance instructional organization and delivery. Instructors should be directly involved in the interpretation and application of outcome results whenever these are applied to evaluating and improving teaching.

What follows is a partial list of strategies commonly used to determine student outcomes. The list is organized in two groups: (1) *micro-level indicators* or assessments conducted in class and (2) *macro-level indicators* or assessments conducted across programs and institutions.

Micro-Level Indicators. Qualitative assessment forms are becoming more common among micro-level indicators. As Biggs (1996) shows, these foster deep rather than surface learning because they elicit students' understanding rather than simple recall, as well as students' ability to apply understanding holistically in authentic contexts. They can also be developmental; they show students' stages of understanding.

Course-Based Tests and Examinations. Tests and examinations are usually designed by the instructors of the particular students whose achievement they assess. Consequently, their validity relies very much on the instructor's test construction ability and biases about what sorts of test responses indicate student knowledge.

Student Products. Normally prepared outside of class, student products include written assignments, portfolios, designs, presentations, functional objects, or art pieces. They demonstrate multiple skills and may reflect students' prior skills and available time as much as the learning developed during a particular course period. But as with course-based tests, faculty use different criteria for judging students' performance, so a valid comparison of student achievement across courses and especially across programs differing markedly in intent and delivery mode is difficult.

Student Performance Observation. Student skills are demonstrated by performing specified tasks in naturalistic, simulated, or laboratory situations. Here the limitations of the evaluator's observational skills, the method of recording, the observer's bias in terms of what comprises successful completion of the task, and the criteria chosen to evaluate the various skills integrated within the demonstration are all suspect. This does not mean that performance observation is inappropriate for determining student outcomes, just that care must be exercised (Fenwick and Parsons, 2000).

In-Class Observation. Many instructors assess student behaviors informally to determine interim outcomes. Class participation is one example. Rating scales are available for the in-class assessment of students' developing competency and knowledge in everything from technical or motor skills to the problem-solving abilities they employ in small group discussions. Instructor bias and the limitations of one observer again present problems for validity. For example, students can demonstrate class participation in many ways other than frequent talking.

Student Reports. Student reports about their experiences can be elicited throughout a course and assessed as interim outcomes. Brookfield (1995) suggests asking learners to write "quick memos" to the instructor at different times during a course. Students can be invited to describe the most confusing part of some instruction they just received, a time in the class they felt successful or frustrated, or the most important new ideas they learned. Obviously, this method is limited by students' level of trust and willingness to disclose, and their perception of their own learning process.

Student Self-Assessment. In self-assessment, students describe the outcomes most meaningful in their learning through approaches such as quick memos or journals in which students record their growth. If a course uses learning portfolios, students may select products they think demonstrate their growing ability. Students may rate their own developing skills using indicators they help design or participate in peer assessment, group self-assessment, and critical reflection exercises (Fenwick and Parsons, 2000). The utility of students' self-assessment depends to a large degree on their understanding of the criteria and its meaningfulness to them, as well as their capacity for critical self-observation.

On-Line Messages. Students participating in on-line discussions in distance courses often post written messages regularly, providing a natural data source for instructors to analyze ongoing student outcomes. Haughey and Anderson (1998) suggest assessment criteria such as frequency, level of engagement, and nature of students' contributions (descriptive, analytic, critical, synthetical, and so on) following instructor questions.

Macro-Level Indicators. As mentioned earlier, these are targeted at the level of entire programs or institutions. They have employed both quantitative and qualitative methods.

Student Interest and Attitude Surveys. Surveys may be carried out informally or formally, within classes, or across the institution. For example, Angelo and Cross (1993) describe a Course-Related Self-Confidence Survey that invites students to rate their level of confidence in learning new and unfamiliar skills in particular areas of a course. Alternatively, large-scale exit surveys or longitudinal surveys may involve student self-assessment of their aspirations, values, communication skills, quantitative skills, critical thinking, personal independence, interpersonal skills, and knowledge of basic facts. The Student Engagement Survey is one of many generic instruments that have been developed and validated and allow for inter-institutional comparisons.

Standardized Achievement Tests. Standardized tests are produced by agencies such as the College Level Examination Program (CLEP) and the American College Testing (ACT) program to measure intellectual skills and knowledge. Most items ask students to interpret and draw generalizations from information presented by deducing, analyzing, and extrapolating. Sometimes these tasks are given to students in a pretest-posttest design in an attempt to assess changes in their knowledge.

The use of mass testing for any purpose besides locating general trends can be strongly contested for many reasons. Standardized tests tend to focus on recall and formulaic problem solving that is isolated from learning contexts. They favor particular learning styles and test-taking capabilities and often are riddled with cultural bias. Such tests also attempt to homogenize meaning making and to separate competencies into disaggregated units of analysis, ignoring how different learners construct knowledge and apply it holistically in particular situations.

Nonetheless, despite strong criticisms and proven limitations, standardized tests are gaining popularity in some jurisdictions as important tools of quality control. Test scores provide the illusion of clear benchmarks. They can be wielded by media and institutional regulators to provide quick, simplistic analyses and comparisons of learning that avoid messy and difficult issues.

Longitudinal Studies. Student outcomes may be assessed through tests delivered in each year of the student's program, and even afterward. Proponents like Pace (1985) explain that longitudinal tests must be controlled for environmental variables and that they work best in the early years after leaving college, when learning and change can be expected to be more intense than at later stages of life. Valuable information can be yielded about the effects on students' outcomes as they change over time, but the process is costly and time consuming.

Alumni Surveys. Alumni surveys tend to focus on success in further education, as well as on students' retrospective evaluation of the benefits of the college and satisfaction with their experience. Individuals' career success and income may also be examined as indicators of the effectiveness of their postsecondary education. Employment information is another source of data about student outcomes. Seppanen (1995) explains how unemployment insurance databases are useful sources of information that can help track graduates' employment history and can be linked directly to the institution's information systems. What behaviors emerging several years after a graduate leaves a college are traceable to a student's higher education experience? And which, if any, are useful indicators of student outcomes that can be linked to teaching?

It is evident that all of these approaches to measuring student outcomes will yield different information, and all have benefits and limitations. The issue concerning the remainder of this chapter is how to select and employ these approaches to productively evaluate teaching. This issue might best be addressed through a combination of macro-level evaluation and micro-level, teacher-directed evaluation, relying heavily on instructor involvement to help determine criteria, method, and interpretation of results. These two approaches are presented consecutively in the following sections.

Micro-Level, Teacher-Directed Evaluation Using Student Outcomes

Teachers themselves are best positioned to interpret student outcomes according to course particularities and apply the results immediately to improve their teaching. This is why micro-level, teacher-directed evaluation is crucial wherever measures of student outcomes are considered. First, instructors can contextualize the outcomes, viewing them in terms of the course topics, pedagogical philosophy and methods, and the nature of the students. Second, instructors can link the outcomes to their teaching purposes. Third, instructors are perhaps in the best position to analyze the subtle links, where they may exist, between teaching behaviors, decisions, and strategies and students' observable or reported indicators of learning. Finally, teacher-directed evaluation emphasizes a positive model of instructors as responsible professionals, not a deficit model of accountability and surveillance.

Bingman and Ebert (2000) describe one example of faculty documenting and analyzing learner outcomes to improve instruction. Small teams of instructors of adult basic education in Kentucky, Virginia, and Tennessee each worked as a collaborative unit to define their purposes for learning, develop skill standards, create ways of mapping successful performance as it might be demonstrated in different contexts, and list activities suitable for sampling student outcomes. Because they were using an action research approach, the methods and process of the project were emergent and collaborative. The instructors met throughout the process to reflect together, interpret what was happening, and make adjustments. Each team also worked with students to experiment with methods of identifying and recording meaningful outcomes.

Bingman and Ebert (2000) report that the collective process itself of carefully analyzing student outcomes and linking it to their methods was responsible for instructors' changing their understanding about aspects of their practice, assessing with greater depth, and working continually to improve their approaches based on the students' outcomes. Another positive result of the project was the extent to which students became involved in defining outcomes: students created goals that they linked to their own outcomes and developed meaningful ways to record their accomplishments.

In another example, Cuttic and others (1999) describe a project undertaken by faculty at Harcum College. Together the faculty designed a year-long assessment project studying the effects of classroom assessment techniques on students' learning outcomes and teaching strategies. The use of the assessment strategies in each classroom was supplemented by monthly meetings of the instructors, journals they kept, and samples of student work, all as part of a teacher-action research project. The instructors often saw immediately where students were having difficulty. Many reflected about what to change in their instruction and discussed the outcome findings with students to generate alternate instructional methods.

Teacher-directed evaluation using student outcomes is potentially very time-intensive. And as these two examples indicate, the process of identifying and assessing student outcomes is not a simple undertaking, nor can it be preplanned and implemented in a linear fashion. Both examples show a group of faculty working collaboratively in an action research process that is inherently messy and unpredictable. However, in each example ways of accurately defining and measuring student outcomes were developed in relation to purposes (both instructor's and students') and the particularities of context. Teaching practice improved, and students became actively involved in determining and interpreting their own assessment. Finally, both examples illustrate the power of teacher-directed evaluation using student outcomes in a collective, where faculty can support one another, draw on each other's strengths, and together tackle a shared problem that might otherwise be borne by each teacher in lonely isolation.

Macro-Level Teacher Evaluation Using Student Outcomes

Although teacher-directed evaluation may be most useful to link student outcomes of a particular course and teacher to the teaching methods, macro-level evaluation of teaching using student outcomes may examine broad trends in terms of a cohort of students. External evaluation normally uses outcomes such as final course grades or results of standardized tests. In isolation, as explained earlier, these have major limitations as indicators of teaching. However, I suggest some approaches incorporating student outcomes in external faculty evaluation that may offer useful information. These approaches should always be combined with teacher-directed evaluation using student outcomes to address context, purposes, and meanings.

Using Student Outcomes as Part of Program Evaluation. Student outcomes such as results of standardized tests, projects, or assignments conducted across groups of students may be useful within the paradigm of program evaluation for problem identification in particular teaching methods, solution development, program improvement, and eventual policy change. Of course, such an approach must account carefully for influences on student outcomes and barriers to validity in mass standardized testing, as described in earlier sections. Delaney (1997) has developed a process that surveys alumni to assess student outcomes in terms of individuals' different program goals, administrators' policy concerns, faculty instructional values, and professional practice standards. These results are combined with assessment of program resources, circumstances influencing the outcomes, and program process factors (such as attendance, support services, and timing or pacing of the program). Each factor is weighted for significance before evaluative judgments are determined. The focus is always on the entire program, with teaching treated as one dimension linked with the others. The study results emphasized the strengths and areas in need of improvement for the institution as a whole.

Combining Multiple Measures of Student Outcomes. Most instructors already realize the importance of assessing student progress through multiple measures, but external evaluation of student outcomes often relies solely on test results or final grades. An outcomes assessment plan relying on a combination of measures at least provides greater insight to students' experiences and learning in particular contexts. For example, Shaeiwitz (1998) describes assessing engineering student outcomes using tests, portfolios, capstone experiences, questionnaires, interviews, job placement, and classroom assessment data.

Alverno College in Milwaukee has been recognized as a pioneer in its integration of multiple measures to provide meaningful feedback to faculty about patterns in student outcomes. Feedback to students is based on eight general abilities integrated throughout the curriculum (such as communication, global perspectives, effective citizenship, and problem solving). Students self-assess their ongoing improvement in these areas using explicit criteria, and faculty together interpret and incorporate outcome information into designing more effective learning experiences (Alverno College Faculty, 1992).

Combining Student Outcome Data with Other Teaching Performance Measures. Zietz, Cochran, and Wilson (1999) combined three data sources:

student grades on a summative test, student evaluations of teaching, and a weighted average of the two. The resulting score for each instructor was compared to that of other instructors and to a score that could be expected for that instructor's class. Ewell (1995) shows that information technologies are more able now to define and track student cohorts, accommodating diverse data from a variety of sources in cost-effective ways. Multiple databases can be linked together, including student record data, institutional surveys, and external data resources such as unemployment insurance wage files.

Involving Faculty. In any external evaluation of teaching, faculty should be involved in choosing the focus, developing criteria, choosing indicators, and interpreting the results. All of the approaches described earlier are limited by their removal from the meanings and relations negotiated among students and their instructors in particular situations. Student outcomes are rooted in these meanings and must be analyzed within them. Or collectively, faculty might conduct an assessment of student outcomes to address a particular teaching strategy they have shared. For example, it is not uncommon for instructors of writing to collaborate on the terms and assessment criteria of an assignment that they all give to their respective students, then grade all the papers as a group to identify trends in student outcomes that can be linked to writing instruction methods.

To be applied fairly to the judgment of teaching, macro-level evaluation based on student outcomes should always involve faculty. The results should be combined with teacher-directed evaluation and ideally with other methods of evaluation such as those described elsewhere in this volume. For these reasons, it is unthinkable to focus just on an individual instructor and rely on findings of an external analysis of test scores or grades of that teacher's students to determine the teacher's proficiency.

Conclusions

When employed carefully and thoughtfully, student outcomes may contribute to judgments of teaching. But learning outcomes are influenced by a complex interplay of factors particular to an institution, teaching context, and student disposition. And because learning is a dynamic, highly idiosyncratic process rooted in social interactions and practices, measurement of these outcomes must employ a variety of methods, both short and long term. For these reasons, micro-level, teacher-directed evaluation of student outcomes should always be combined with macro-level evaluation, and faculty should be involved in developing criteria and data collection methods for macro-level evaluation methods. In addition, the judgment of teaching should be conducted within a process of overall program evaluation that examines many dimensions affecting student learning outcomes.

Whether focused generally on overall program improvement or specifically on faculty development, student outcome information appears to be most productively used by faculty working as a group toward a collective vision. The goal is building sufficient trust among teachers that they are willing to open up and share areas of weakness and strength together and work collegially to address such issues.

Evaluation processes that are productive, valid, and reliable are usually labor-intensive and time consuming. A note must be made that collecting meaningful data about student outcomes may demand increased paperwork from instructors already feeling overburdened. For this reason, the use of student outcomes for evaluating teaching and programs should be sparing and periodic rather than continuous and dependent on time, resources, and recognition from the institution.

Finally, any method of judging teaching is problematic when it becomes the sole measure. An effective program of ongoing faculty development should employ student outcomes in combination with student evaluations of the course, peer classroom observation, peer evaluation of course syllabus and materials, and instructors' self-assessments. The most important thing is that student outcome information be ultimately used to support and improve teaching, not contribute to faculty stress, fear, and alienation in an age obsessed with accountability.

References

Alverno College Faculty. *Liberal Learning at Alverno College.* Milwaukee: Wisc.: Alverno Productions, 1992.

Angelo, T., and Cross, P. *Classroom Assessment Techniques: A Handbook for College Teachers.* San Francisco: Jossey-Bass, 1993.

Astin, A. W. *Four Critical Years: Effects of College on Beliefs, Attitudes, and Knowledge.* San Francisco: Jossey-Bass, 1978.

Banta, T. W. (ed.). *Implementing Outcomes Assessment: Promise and Perils* San Francisco: Jossey-Bass, 1988.

Biggs, J "Assessing Learning Quality: Reconciling Institutional, Staff, and Educational Demands." *Assessment and Evaluation in Higher Education,* (Mar. 1996), 21, 5–15.

Bingman, M. B., and Ebert, O. *I've Come A Long Way: Learner-Identified Outcomes of Participation in Adult Literacy Programs.* Cambridge, Mass.: National Center for the Study of Adult Learning and Literacy, 2000.

Britzman, D. P. *Lost Subjects, Contested Objects: Toward a Psychoanalytic Inquiry of Learning.* New York: SUNY Press, 1998.

Brookfield, S. D. *Becoming a Critically Reflective Teacher.* San Francisco: Jossey-Bass, 1995.

Brown, J., and Duguid, P "Stolen Knowledge." In H. McLellan (ed.), *Situated Learning Perspectives.* Englewood Cliffs, N.J.. Educational Technology Publications, 1996.

Cuttic, N., Hilosky, A., Perkinson, J., Reynolds, P. R., and Sylvis, R. "Using Classroom Assessment Techniques to Empower Teachers: A View From the Faculty." *Journal of Applied Research in the Community College,* 1999, 6(2), 87–95.

Delaney, A. M. "Quality Assessment of Professional Degree Programs." *Research in Higher Education,* 1997, 38, 241–264.

Ewell, P. T. "Working Over Time. The Evolution of Longitudinal Student Tracking Data Bases." In P. T. Ewell (ed.), *Student Tracking: New Techniques, New Demands*. San Francisco: Jossey-Bass, 1995.

Fenwick, T., and Parsons, J. *The Art of Evaluation: A Handbook for Educators and Trainers*. Toronto: Thompson Educational Publishing, 2000.

Giroux, H., and McLaren, P. (eds.). *Between Borders: Pedagogy and the Politics of Cultural Studies*. New York: Routledge, 1994.

Haughey, M., and Anderson, T. *Networked Learning: The Pedagogy on the Internet*. Montreal/Toronto: Cheneliere/McGraw-Hill, 1998.

Karpiak, I. "Ghosts in the Wilderness: Problems and Priorities of Faculty at Mid-Career and Mid-Life." *Canadian Journal of Higher Education*, 1996, 26(3), 49–78.

Kember, D., and Gow, L. "Orientations to Teaching and Their Effect on the Quality of Student Learning." *Journal of Higher Education*, 1994, 65, 58–74.

Kirschner, D., and Witson, J. (eds). *Situated Cognition: Social, Semiotic, and Psychological Perspectives*. Mahway, N.J.: Erlbaum, 1997.

Lave, J., and Wenger, E. *Situated Learning: Legitimate Peripheral Participation*. New York: Cambridge Press, 1991.

Pace, C. R "Perspectives and Problems in Student Outcomes Research." In P. T. Ewell (ed.), *Assessing Educational Outcomes*. San Francisco: Jossey-Bass, 1985.

Ramsden, P., and Entwistle, N. J. "Effects of Academic Departments on Students' Approaches to Studying." *British Journal of Educational Psychology*, 1981, 51, 368–383.

Seppanen, L. J. "Linkages to the World of Employment." In P. T. Ewell (ed.), *Student Tracking: New Techniques, New Demands* San Francisco: Jossey-Bass, 1995.

Sergiovanni. T. J., and Starratt, R. J. *Supervision: A Redefinition*. (7th ed.) Boston: McGraw-Hill, 2002.

Shaeiwitz, J. A. "Outcomes Assessment Methods." *Chemical Engineering Education*, 1998, 32, 128–131, 145.

Trowler, P. R. *Academics Responding to Change: New Higher Education Frameworks and Academic Cultures*. Buckingham, U.K.: Society for Research into Higher Education and Open University Press, 1998.

Wenger, E. *Communities of Practice: Learning, Meaning and Identity*. Cambridge. Cambridge University Press, 1998.

Zietz, J., Cochran, H. H., Jr., and Wilson, M. L. "Evaluating Instructional Effectiveness." Paper presented at the Annual Meeting of the Mid-South Educational Research Association, Point Clear, Ala., Nov. 1999. (ED 435 750)

TARA J. FENWICK *is assistant professor of adult education in the Department of Educational Policy Studies at the University of Alberta.*

8

The accreditation of faculty as teaching professionals is one way to provide standardized criteria for the evaluation of teaching. In the United Kingdom, great strides are being made in this direction.

Teaching Evaluation and Accreditation

Liz Beaty

In this chapter, I use recent developments in teacher accreditation in the United Kingdom as a case study through which to consider the implications for evaluating teaching and the changing identity of academics. The evaluation of teaching implies a notion of good teaching and a view that it can be improved. On what basis is this judgment made? What counts as good teaching? How do we know when someone who is given the job of teaching is capable of doing it well? The answers to such questions are currently in focus as higher education goes through a period of rapid change. I describe the development of professional status through the accreditation of teaching in higher education.

The Need for Accreditation of Teaching in Higher Education

New faculty in higher education are entering a different world from that of traditional academic scholars. Beginning teachers must look to the national and international context in a way that is unprecedented, and they must realize the transience of their knowledge and the narrow nature of their expertise. Universities are no longer simply a finishing school for the few but must respond to the expectations of governments and citizens for the continued and sustainable development of students, so faculty must provide students with opportunities to develop lifelong learning skills. Moreover, managing the teaching of traditional disciplinary content and expertise is becoming increasingly difficult as fewer students have predictable prior knowledge or predictable futures.

New Directions for Teaching and Learning, no 88, Winter 2001 © John Wiley & Sons, Inc

The need for a benchmark of good practice in teaching in higher education comes from two sets of factors. The first has to do with the greater demands made on higher education through

- The growth and development of information technology and the consequent need for the management of information
- The widening access to and growth of distance education
- Globalization
- Declining resources, coupled with increased stakeholder demands for involvement in setting the goals of higher education
- The view of "student as customer"
- Increasing numbers of mature adult students
- The need to foster lifelong learning

The second set of factors has to do with the importance of understanding how adults learn and the need to apply what we know from adult education to higher education practice. Specifically, we are challenged by

- The move away from knowledge transmission to information management and active learning
- The call for the integration of academic and business worlds in experiential and work-based learning
- The demand for student-centered learning and resource-based instruction
- The importance of recognizing individual differences in learning styles and developing the ability to teach in radically different modes
- The need to incorporate new developments in learning technology

These two sets of factors interact to provide a new imperative for change in higher education.

In times of radical change, most companies invest up to 15 percent of their turnover in staff development. In higher education, such spending has traditionally been on research through sabbatical leaves and grants to attend conferences. In the United Kingdom at the present time, there is a move to both increase the total amount of resources committed to staff development and to rebalance its focus—in particular to provide training for teaching. An important issue then is what should be included in a training course for teachers. How do we decide what good teaching is? The move toward accreditation for teachers comes from this need to define and identify the basis on which teaching is provided in higher education.

Professional Identity and Professionalism

Most professional groups have at least two features in common: they have (1) clear training routes toward qualifications that give entry to the profession and (2) a professional body that defines entry standards, a code of

ethics, and sanctions for misdemeanors. The qualifications needed to practice in the profession are specified, and courses that educate to this standard
are given accreditation through scrutiny by the appropriate professional
body. New professionals must gain a certificate of entry to the profession
through a course of study, normally followed by a specified period of supervised practice. Accreditation is the main way in which entry to a profession
is controlled and by which clients, employers, and other stakeholders can
recognize bona fide practitioners.

There are a number of good reasons for developing mechanisms to control standards in the professions. First, it is imperative that clients using the
services of professionals can have a reasonable amount of trust in their competence. Rogue practitioners can do great damage, not only to their clients
but also indirectly to the reputation of the profession as a whole. All people
who practice a particular profession have as much reason as clients do to
support accreditation processes that guarantee at least a minimum level of
training. Second, professional groups gain control over their practice
through discipline within the group. Thus professional autonomy allows
practitioners responsibility for standards. Being part of a controlled professional group guarantees high status, which brings added benefits for the
identity of the individual. On the downside, professional status can also lead
to restrictive practices and falsely inflated pay rates and fees.

Although many professional groups control their own standards ini-
tially, government has become increasingly involved in conferring and controlling certain aspects of professional status. This is particularly true where
government provides the resources for training. In the case of school teachers, for example, governments generally control training standards because
the role of teacher is seen to be crucial to the ordered functioning of society. Status, then, has become as much about societal control as about professional power and autonomy.

Academic Identities

Higher education is in the business of educating many professional groups
(including teachers), and the qualifications that students gain on graduation are usually an essential part of the accreditation of professionals. So it
is rather strange that the idea of accreditation for teachers in higher education is relatively new. Although some countries have a history of courses
being provided to support faculty development, there has been little attempt
at consistency of this provision. Nor has there been much interest from
external sources in the quality of such courses. Until recently, most training of teachers in higher education was ad hoc, voluntary, and unlikely to
result in any qualification. Why is this the case, and what has changed to bring
teacher accreditation so much into focus?

One answer is to be found in the identity of academics. When asked,
most academics define themselves through their discipline. For example, they

tend to say, "I am a biologist" rather than "I teach biology." The usual route into academia is through a higher degree in the subject or practice in a professional area. The new teacher has become a faculty member after apprenticeship in the study of the discipline. The profession, if there is one, is as an academic and not a pedagogue. It is also true that many academics have gained accreditation from professional bodies associated with the practice of their discipline; medical faculty, for example, are almost always accredited doctors, academic engineers usually have accreditation as chartered engineers, and so forth. Faculty have therefore seen their professional status emanating from their discipline rather than from their role as *teachers* of the discipline.

Many academics would argue that they are not, in fact, teachers but rather professors of their particular subject. In this view, being a knowledgeable and active researcher is seen as the key task, and teaching students is a sideline. Good teaching, where it is defined, is seen as the enthusiastic transmission of knowledge about the subject with the aim of encouraging students to become part of the community of practice this subject involves. The traditional view is of a young adult learning independently in a vibrant academic community where faculty are only one aspect of the rich resources available. The student is part of a community of scholars and is expected to learn by what the English call "reading for a degree."

By this analysis there is no need for any training in teaching, and pedagogy is left behind at the precollege level. Students are apprentices, studying with the professor and learning from the role model. Although this may work for the few students who go on to be professors themselves, most undergraduates do not have such a goal. In a mass system of higher education, few students progress beyond a bachelor's degree; fewer still become academics. Modern university students, it is argued, do not need an apprenticeship so much as a basic grounding in disciplinary knowledge and, crucially, development of cognitive and transferable skills to enable them to take on future employment in a diverse range of graduate jobs.

Expansion, Diversity, and Lifelong Learning

In Chapter Nine, Robert Cannon looks closely at the role of stakeholders in the evaluation of teaching. In this section I point to why different stakeholders have backed the move toward the accreditation of teachers in higher education.

In many countries, higher education is needed to cater to an increasing proportion of the school-leaving population. The challenge of the modern world is seen as the need for constant updating, with professional development being continuous rather than simply foundational. In this new world, higher education must respond to an ever-increasing diversity of learners with demands for relevant, timely, and carefully crafted just-in-time learning opportunities. A full-time, three- or four-year degree is becoming a luxury few can afford and governments are no longer prepared to fund. Much more is being asked of teaching in higher education; therefore, more is being required of those who teach. The current focus on higher education as a provider of skills for the knowledge society and the need for a more educated workforce has led to a call for lifelong learning. Along with this has come an increased pressure on resources and an emphasis on quality issues and accountability.

The move to a mass system of higher education has been an impetus for a change in the definition of good teaching. Evidence from student feedback, for example, indicates that many top professors, rather than being excellent in communicating enthusiasm for their subject, are deadly boring teachers. They are criticized by students for being distracted by their own narrow, specialized interests and dismissive of the needs of undergraduate novice learners. Being a good researcher, it seems, does not guarantee that one will be a good teacher. There is still a debate on exactly what the relationship between teaching and research is and should be, but the evidence that the quality of one necessarily leads to quality in the other in a causal way has been roundly debunked. Indeed, abundant evidence shows that there is no correlation between teaching effectiveness and research productivity (Hattie and Marsh, 1996). A better view of the relationship, however, may be to see that teachers' conceptions of teaching and of research importantly shape the connection between them through notions of scholarship and critical thinking (Brew, 1999).

At first glance it appears obvious that the more experience someone has working as a teacher, the better teacher that person would be. But it is possible to simply have one year of experience repeated twenty times over twenty years. Hence experience, although extremely useful and developmental, cannot guarantee good teaching. Furthermore, untrained teachers can be forgiven for their narrow and uninspired view of teaching because their views are largely based on their own experiences as undergraduates! We can describe higher education as one of the last cottage industries; lecturers are happy to plod along with an amateur craft model of working, which is rife with inefficiency and lack of accountability (Elton, 1994). The move to the accreditation of teaching has been driven by multiple stakeholders: students, employers, educational developers, governments, and even parents.

In recent years the pressure on resources, along with the need for evaluation evidence and for accountability, has brought about an increasing need for universities to put more effort into staff development of all kinds. Along with this, the calls from academic development specialists for teacher development have begun to be heeded. It is now recognized that faculty need support to develop the required skills.

The Development of Teacher Accreditation in the United Kingdom: A Case Study

In the United Kingdom, the National Union of Students has argued strongly for accreditation in order to force a focus on teaching as opposed to the overriding emphasis on research. Their report to the National Commission on Higher Education (NCIHE, 1997) included a strong argument for compulsory training of graduate teaching assistants and full-time lecturers in teaching practice. Students have for many years been dissatisfied with the quality of teaching. As they have become more preoccupied with a need to gain employment, this view has become more forceful. Students' views have been supported by their parents, who are having to provide increasing financial support for university study. The recent move to levy tuition fees directly from students has caused greater pressure for accountability in teaching quality.

From the point of view of the politicians, the push for quality has been reinforced by moves toward greater accountability throughout the public sector. Higher education was unlikely to be spared from the overarching concerns of government for efficiency in public spending. Although the British government wished to expand higher education, it did not want to invest in this expansion in the same proportion that it had for the smaller, more elite higher education system. Government was looking for a way to get more and spend less. Hence the relentless diminishing resource per student needed to be matched by measures of quality to safeguard standards. Meanwhile, institutional managers were sharply aware that pressure on staff needed to be matched by development opportunities that would help achieve better quality.

Educational developers could not believe their good fortune. After years in the wilderness, ignored by all but the most needy or the most devoted of teachers, they suddenly found themselves the center of attention and the hope of the sector. Did they have a response to this need? Did they know how to define good teaching and how to bring it about through staff development?

The SEDA Model of Teacher Accreditation

In early 1990, the Staff and Educational Development Association (SEDA) was busy designing an accreditation scheme for teachers in higher education that was both influential and incredibly timely. The original motivation for this scheme was to encourage institutions to commit resources to staff development. The rationale was that if a benchmark could be established that set out what was required as an outcome from professional training, then institutional managers were more likely to commit resources to it. If the local educational developer was able point to a standard that others were working to meet and say that it took a year of part-time in-service training to reach that standard, then institutional managers could no longer get away with the half-day induction courses they had previously argued were adequate.

The accreditation scheme, therefore, came out of an aim to create a benchmark and to avoid each institution reinventing the wheel in designing its own version of a professional course. The scheme was devised through researching the current practice in different institutions. The original vision was to provide an ideal but typical course, designed to show best practice in professional training for teaching in higher education. However, the various approaches in use at the time were so diverse and the individual contexts of institutions so powerful that this proved too difficult. Instead SEDA produced an outline set of outcomes and values that any program should be able to meet. This was designed as a template against which courses of staff development could be matched.

The SEDA scheme outlines a set of learning outcomes and a set of underlying values and principles. Courses or programs of faculty development that can demonstrate that they support and assess teachers using this framework are recognized within the scheme. Teachers who successfully complete a recognized program gain a Certificate of Accreditation as a teacher in higher education. The scheme does not set out a particular course structure, academic level, or assessment process, but many courses within the scheme are at the postgraduate level; they are work-based and take about one year of part-time study. The usual pattern is for students to be assessed on actual teaching practice and reflective narratives, brought together as a teaching portfolio.

The scheme has been running since 1992 and currently has fifty-eight recognized programs. It has been successful in sharing practice across different universities, and it is possible to describe typical features of such courses, such as the use of teaching observation as evidence of good practice, portfolio assessment, and the use of action learning and mentoring to provide ongoing teacher support (Beaty, 1997).

During the 1990s, the SEDA Teacher Accreditation Scheme became a benchmark. Over the decade, almost half of the institutions of higher education in the United Kingdom had programs recognized under the scheme, and the graduates from these programs received a SEDA Accreditation Certificate alongside their institutional qualification. The scheme was also used in various international programs as a benchmark and a spur to local developments. Universities in Australia, Hong Kong, New Zealand, Singapore, and Sri Lanka now have SEDA-recognized programs. The scheme was also endorsed by name in the recommendations of the recent National Commission (Dearing) report, which stated that training and accreditation for higher education teaching should be introduced and recommended the establishment of an Institute for Learning and Teaching.

The teaching unions were also interested in this development. They wanted to endorse professional standards for their members, not least to protect their professional status and salary position. The Association of University Teachers (AUT) and SEDA were influential together in establishing the continued debate on the nature of the national accreditation framework and in supporting the moves for creation of the Institute for Learning and Teaching (ILT). This new body is intended to be the professional body for teachers in higher education. Over its first year of operation the institute has built its own accreditation framework, and almost all U.K. universities have signed up to the standard.

The United Kingdom is still some way from having a fully implemented accreditation program for university staff, and although many programs of training have been developed, they are taken by relatively few new staff.

Hence many faculty remain untrained, despite an easy route to membership of ILT for experienced teachers. Recruitment to the new institute has been slow, and the training model is still contested. At this time, it is not clear what will happen in the longer term, and yet there is a growing consensus within the universities and in stakeholder groups that teacher accreditation is a necessary and important way to evaluate and support the development of standards in teaching.

Accreditation and the Outcomes for Learners

Teaching portfolios from courses leading to accreditation often include self-assessments that testify to the developmental effect of such experience on teaching. The portfolios also include student ratings that generally demonstrate improvement as the course progresses. Student unions are very keen to support such training because they clearly believe it has enhanced the student experience in higher education. Administrators clearly support the move to accreditation, and it is becoming a common feature of U.K. higher education staff development policy to have such courses as compulsory elements for new faculty. Recent reports of institutional quality have commented favorably on the courses' effects on teaching competence (QAA, 2000).

The various stakeholders agree that this type of staff development leads to greater effectiveness. However, there is still an intransigence in some quarters and a lack of incentives for better teaching through the promotion system, which still tends to rely heavily on research criteria. Working only with new staff can have drawbacks because they lack power and influence and can easily be turned aside from good practice by the greater power of habit and by the control of senior staff who do not share the ideas or philosophy. This is becoming much less of a problem as the courses themselves and the general idea of accreditation become normal practice. In sum, although the accreditation developments in the United Kingdom have been broadly welcomed and successful, there is still a long way to go before accreditation and training are fully accepted, and we are still far from having all our faculty become professionally accredited.

Developments Around the World

Training provision for teaching in higher education varies tremendously, and much can be learned by looking at what is offered around the world. Internationally, courses have been aimed at different groups of staff and have had different flavors and emphases. Moreover, the balance between educational theory and practical technique varies considerably.

In the United States and Canada there has been a focus on the development of new faculty for many years. These mainly younger staff tend to be graduate students in Ph.D. programs who undertake teaching duties as part of a wider apprenticeship into academia. Their training is often conducted by educational development staff and may conclude with the production of a teaching portfolio. Courses offered to this group tend to emphasize such skills as classroom management and teaching methods. Although such programs have been well received, for the most part only a small number of graduate students and prospective faculty have been involved.

In Canada, the Society for Teaching and Learning in Higher Education (the sister organization to SEDA in the United Kingdom) runs a fellowship award program, which is sponsored by 3M Canada. In 1994 a group of 3M teaching fellows articulated an ethical code for teaching in higher education, which sets out a succinct description of an ethical framework and includes examples of when such a code could be deemed to have been broken. As a way of describing professional practice this document is very useful and, alongside the SEDA statement of outcomes and values, gives an authoritative outline of ethical practice against which professional teaching can be evaluated (STLHE, 1996).

In the United Kingdom the focus is on new academic staff, and courses are compulsory in many institutions. They tend to be based on a reflective-practice model of experiential learning, which is supported by training workshops. For other countries, such as Australia, the intended audience is experienced staff who are in control of curriculum development. Here the curriculum is more theoretical and more focused on educational research.

In all cases the goal is to improve student learning through the skilled (and knowledgeable) intervention of teachers. Professional ethics, values, and principles are included, along with consciousness raising and skill training in practical educational methods and an understanding of learning and curriculum design through scholarship. Some programs aimed at more experienced staff are based on teaching innovation and action research.

In some developing countries the need to take a global perspective and the need for an international benchmark are even more imperative. Global competitiveness and the continued brain drain mean that the provision of higher education has to be constantly upgraded. The employability of graduates is essential for these nations, and they look to higher education to provide the relevant skills. Even more than for the rich western world, developing countries need their higher education systems to be forward looking and up to date in the development of a skilled and creative workforce. For these reasons, teacher accreditation that is based on an established international model has proved very attractive, and hard-won funding has been used to gain accreditation for staff development programs. The benefits have been noticeable in terms of the greater confidence of staff and positive responses from students and employers.

An international benchmark also proves useful for the employment of academic staff across national borders. When institutions can understand the nature of a qualification because it is benchmarked against a recognizable standard, there is greater opportunity for international cooperation and transfer.

In sum, we are seeing a growing consensus that teaching involves specialized knowledge and skills that must be developed through courses of professional development. Such programs should meet agreed-on professional standards, and the successful completion of such programs should be acknowledged through professional status.

Issues in Professionalization

The professionalization of teaching has been criticized for a number of reasons.

Loss of Autonomy. Professionalization results in the loss of autonomy for faculty. It is seen by some as part of a creeping managerialism and control by the state. It certainly affects the identity of faculty. To see ourselves as teachers rather than as subject area experts is a fundamental shift for many, even though for many years unions (such as at the U.K. Association of University Teachers) have used the word *teacher* in their title.

Cost. Although governments and managers of institutions have an incentive to develop the teaching skills of academics, there is a disincentive in how much this could cost. Making teaching in higher education a professional role would involve adding to the cost of research degrees the cost of teacher training, and this will not be taken on lightly. Yet providing resources for teacher accreditation must be taken seriously if it is to be a lasting development.

Responsibility. Other important questions include, Who is responsible for training teachers in higher education? and What is the nature of their professional expertise? Educational developers have taken on this task, but as a group they themselves lack consistent qualifications. Courses for teacher development in the United Kingdom tend to have many of the same features, due to the sharing of practice through the accreditation scheme, but those who teach the teachers have many different positions and roles. In response to such challenges, this group is itself moving to professionalize, and the first qualification for educational development specialists is being offered in the form of a SEDA Fellowship. Thus the professionalization of one group spawns the professionalization of another.

Conclusions

Evaluation requires a set of criteria by which we judge whether or not something is good or effective. Over the decades during which the evaluation of teaching has remained a contentious issue in higher education, the absence of such criteria has been a roadblock in our thinking. A move toward the accreditation of teaching in higher education as a profession is one way of providing standardized criteria for evaluation. In the United Kingdom, the development of such a model is well under way. In this development, it is important that the focus remain on students and their learning.

References

Beaty, L. "The Professional Development of Teachers in Higher Education: Structures, Methods, and Responsibilities." *Innovations in Education and Training International,* 1997, *35,* 99–107.

Brew, A. "Research and Teaching: Changing Relationships in a Changing Context." *Studies in Higher Education.,* 1999, *24,* 291–301.

Elton, L. *Management of Teaching and Learning: Towards Change in Universities.* London: Committee of Vice Chancellors and Principles, 1994.

Hattie, J., and Marsh, H. W. "The Relationship Between Research and Teaching: A Meta Analysis." *Review of Educational Research.,* 1996, *66,* 507–542.

National Commission on Higher Education. *Higher Education for Life Long Learning, Summary Report.* London: Her Majesty's Stationery Office, 1997.

QAA Quality Assessment Review Reports, 2000. [http.//www.qaa.ac.uk]

Staff and Educational Development Association. *The Teacher Accreditation Scheme.* Birmingham, England: Staff and Educational Development Association, 1996.

Society for Teaching and Learning in Higher Education. *Professional Ethics for Teachers in Higher Education.* North York, Ontario: Society for Teaching and Learning in Higher Education, 1996.

LIZ BEATY *is director of the Centre for Higher Education Development at Coventry University, England.*

*Increasing demand for accountability for teaching in
departments, programs, and entire institutions is shifting
the focus of evaluation away from individual instructors
in classroom settings to the broader context of whole
programs, departments, and institutions.*

Broadening the Context for Teaching Evaluation

Robert Cannon

The evaluation of teaching in colleges and universities has primarily focused
on the use of student ratings of individual instructors in classroom settings.
Data from these evaluations have been used for both summative and formative purposes. But there are increasing demands for accountability in teaching at the level of departments, programs, and entire institutions. This chapter
discusses some of the approaches that have been used for these purposes.

In a scathing introduction to teacher evaluation that he wrote more
than twenty years ago, Michael Scriven (1981) touched on several issues
that have as much relevance today as they did then. He asserted that
"teacher evaluation is a disaster" because "the practices are shoddy and the
principles are unclear" (p. 244). He claimed that practice did not reflect current knowledge and that pressure to reform was coming from outside the
universities, specifically government and the courts.

Seeking clarity about the principles of evaluation is a necessary step to
begin to address the accusation of engaging in shoddy practices. This is not as
straightforward as it may seem because the domain of evaluation is extremely
complex (Johnson and Ryan, 2000). According to Scriven (1991), evaluation
is an analytical process of determining the merit, worth, or value of something
and involves two main dimensions: (1) gathering data and then (2) using data
for judgment and decision making with respect to agreed-on standards.

Scriven's criticisms reflect several important contextual issues. We cannot assume that teaching only involves instructors working as autonomous
individuals in teacher-centered classrooms dominated by the lecture and
class discussion methods. Yet if we look at many of the formal evaluation
systems in current use, we might conclude that this is the dominant and
perhaps desired teaching paradigm in universities.

NEW DIRECTIONS FOR TEACHING AND LEARNING, no 88, Winter 2001 © John Wiley & Sons, Inc

In fact, approaches to teaching are increasingly shaped by changing needs, expectations, resources, organizational structures, and conceptions of the teaching process itself (Glassick, Huber, and Maeroff, 1997; Kember, 1997; Pratt, 1997). Over the past two decades, focused efforts to improve teaching through research, publication, consultancy, evaluation, and professional development have yielded a great variety of ways to think about learning and teaching in universities. This has been partly a response to external pressure. Governments are taking a close interest in higher education and are using mechanisms such as performance-based funding to drive change.

A gradual reorientation of policies and practices toward learning rather than teaching (Barr and Tagg, 1995; Norris and Malloch, 1997) has had implications for evaluation practices. It is recognized that if we are serious about the quality of student learning and its outcomes, then evaluators must accept that they have a significant role to play in shaping the learning and teaching environment of universities. They can do this by aligning evaluation policy and practice with institutional goals (Biggs, 1996, 1999). In a contextually aligned system the institutional mission, strategic objectives, educational methods, assessment, and evaluation approaches are congruent. So, for example, any institution that declares its strategic commitment to student-centered, lifelong learning would rigorously employ learning and teaching methods and assessment procedures that reflect this commitment. An example of nonalignment might be for an institution claiming a commitment to lifelong learning to emphasize teacher-centered methods such as large group lectures, formal examinations, the electronic delivery of copious instructional materials, and the widespread use of student ratings of instructors' presentation skills.

Of course, the autonomous, teacher-centered construct was never a true representation of all teaching in higher education. It is likely to be even less true in the future, as the diversity of approaches to learning and teaching expands in response to research and development (Centra, 2000). The context for teaching has changed in other ways, too. One imperative for many universities has been to keep a keen eye on the competitive business environment, and this change has been accompanied by the introduction of several evaluation and quality assurance tools, such as benchmarking and audit, that have their origins in the business world (Alstete, 1996; Holmes and Brown, 2000).

Although we think of teaching as a solitary activity, in one sense instructors in higher education rarely work alone. More usually, they belong to an academic department and hence are part of a team with other instructors and ancillary support staff. Although individuals make important contributions to the work of the team, and these contributions can be identified and evaluated, it is nevertheless true that the experience of students attending a university over the three or four years of an undergraduate degree program is shaped by the sum of the contributions of several different team members. From this perspective, a valid evaluation of teaching should focus less on individual instructors and more on the ways in which these contributions come together in students' experience of their program as a whole.

The Focus and Level of Evaluation

In the past, the relatively narrow focus on student ratings of instructors has to some extent masked the wide range of levels and contexts in which learning and teaching occur and are susceptible to evaluation. All too often, a method of teacher evaluation devised for one context has been applied uncritically in other, different contexts, providing an example of Scriven's "shoddy practice."

One example is the use of teacher-focused questionnaires in problem-based learning courses. In problem-based learning, the focus of activity is on what students are doing in relation to the learning environment that is designed for them, and ratings of instructor performance may be completely inappropriate. Items on the evaluation instrument may refer to largely non-relevant matters such as lecturing skills. Even worse, instructors may feel pressured to behave in ways dictated by the survey instrument rather than the program's goals and strategies. The shoddy practice in this example is non-alignment of the evaluation approach with the goals of learning and teaching.

Some of the levels for evaluation and the corresponding methodological approaches are listed in Table 9.1. The remainder of this chapter will focus on the levels that are indicative of the broadening context in which the evaluation of teaching is now taking place.

Performance Indicators for Teaching. The conflicting pressures to expand higher education within severe funding constraints have contributed to worldwide demands for increased efficiency and accountability (Linke, 1991). The term *performance indicators* is now widely used to describe many of the evaluative approaches listed in the lower half of Exhibit 9.1.

The main advantage of having a system of performance indicators is their utility in enabling comparisons with peers, assessing change over time,

Table 9.1. Levels of Evaluation

Focus of Evaluation	Indicators of Teaching Performance
Individual instructor or teacher	Student evaluation
Teaching teams	Peer evaluation
Course, unit, or program of study	Course Experience Questionnaire
Academic department	Portfolios Audits Benchmarking
Institution	Portfolios Benchmarking Ranking

or measuring achievements against a stated goal (Gaither, Nedwek, and Neal, 1994). Many of the evaluative procedures discussed in this chapter, such as the student ratings of teaching and the Course Experience Questionnaire (CEQ), are examples of performance indicators. But the term is sometimes used in confusing ways that obfuscate rather than clarify.

Indicators are management tools used for presenting information about some characteristic of teaching and learning. They are an adjunct to qualitative judgment but no substitute for it. Indicators can reduce complexity, sometimes to the degree of a misleadingly simple quantitative measure. Indicators can also be used to measure the context of teaching itself, such as student and faculty characteristics and the availability of teaching resources.

There are essentially three kinds of indicators (Cuenin, in Cave, Hanney, Kogan, and Trevett, 1997). Simple indicators, expressed in the form of absolute figures, are intended to provide a relatively objective representation of a situation and can help in the interpretation of other indicators. An example of a simple indicator would be "enrollment in 1999 was 17,654 students." Second, a performance indicator can serve as a relative measure of achievement by providing a point of reference, such as a goal, standard, or comparator. An example would be, "the graduation rate in 1999 was 95 percent" (that is, of one hundred entrants, ninety-five completed successfully). Performance indicators are important when relative judgments are to be made. Finally, general indicators may include peer reviews, surveys, accreditation panel reports, and the like.

Performance indicators of teaching are being used in several ways. Governments use them to inform policy and to allocate resources. For example, they are integral to the notion of performance-based funding of teaching: the notion that measured performance in teaching can be used as a management strategy to both improve and reward evidence of high-quality teaching.

Performance indicators are also used increasingly by the media to construct rankings of universities. Dobson (2000) showed how *The Times, Financial Times, U.S. News and World Report,* and *Asiaweek* constructed their rankings using a wide range of indicators. What is particularly striking when the teaching and learning indicators are examined is that out of thirty indicators there was only one direct measure of learning. This had the particularly opaque descriptor "mean teaching quality, assessment subject scores" and was used by two of the four publications. There was no direct measure of teaching quality; a range of indirect performance indicators was used, including student-teacher ratios (used by all the publications), class size, and even median academic salary (used by two of the publications). Given the potential influence these publications have on very large international audiences, it is a concern that they adopt such a shallow approach, sustained by very indirect indicators of teaching and learning effectiveness.

The Portfolio, Dossier, or Professional Profile. Whereas student ratings of teaching tend toward an atomistic approach to evaluation ("the instructor was well organized," "the tests were fair," and so on), the portfolio stands in contrast as a way of bringing together in one holistic document an integrated range of evidence about teaching. A well-compiled portfolio includes accounts of the context in which teaching occurs and is an excellent example of "alignment." As a summary of teaching accomplishments, the compiler of the portfolio can address the goals to be achieved and present a relevant selection of evidence in support of those goals. This alignment aids the reliability and validity of the subsequent processes of judgment.

The concept of the teaching portfolio has been borrowed from fields such as architecture and art where collections of work have been traditionally integrated and presented. Originating in Canada as the "teaching dossier" (Shore and others, 1986), the concept of the portfolio has been successfully applied at a variety of levels, ranging from student learning portfolios (Biggs, 1999) to portfolios that measure the accomplishments of an entire organization (Hicks, 2000; Mullins and Cannon, 1992).

Portfolios generally have three main elements. First, there is a statement of goals and responsibilities, which provides the contextual basis against which judgments can be made. Second, there is an outline of major achievements, including a statement of philosophy of teaching and learning, in relation to institutional goals and plans. The third part of a portfolio is the summarized evidence of achievements and effectiveness. Sources such as Shore and others (1986) and Edgerton, Hutchings, and Quinlan (1991) give extensive lists of items illustrating achievement that might be appropriate for inclusion in a portfolio. They include, for example, the products of good teaching, descriptions of steps taken to evaluate and improve effectiveness, information from students and peers, evidence of invitations to teach for outside agencies, and contributions to the teaching literature. The term *professional profile* has been coined by Glassick, Huber, and Maeroff (1997) to describe this tripartite form of organization.

The portfolio concept has been applied, not just for individual faculty but at the level of the academic department. The departmental portfolio was originally conceived as an approach to allocating resources to departments and avoiding the use of simplistic, unitary measures of teaching quality (Mullins and Cannon, 1991). Its component parts were to be contextual information about the department, evidence of learning outcomes at a high level of generalization, student evaluation of their course experience (an idea later taken up in the CEQ), evidence of innovation, and evidence of contributions by faculty to the development of teaching quality.

Initial trials of the departmental portfolio were unsuccessful because the context of resource allocation encouraged a defensive and minimalist approach. But the trial did point to valuable lessons concerning implementation. A later application of the concept at the University of Western Australia—the "Ensuring Teaching Quality—Best Practice Pathways"—had much more positive outcomes and eventually led to awards for teaching quality and the dissemination of information provided in portfolios about good practice within the University (Hicks, 2000).

Portfolios have also been used in assessing teaching at the national level. For example, in 1993 Australian universities participating in a national quality audit process initiated by the federal government submitted portfolios of their work. The portfolios were limited in length to twenty pages of evidential material and included information about student and faculty characteristics, provision of feedback on teaching, links with industry, postgraduate teaching, instructional innovations, and international benchmarking. The teaching and learning portfolios, supported by material in appendixes and peer site visits, were used as evidence to make judgments about institutional merit for the allocation of funding to support further quality development.

Despite their increasing acceptance, portfolios are not without limitations. One issue is the problem of portfolios lacking selectivity and coherence and thereby placing considerable demands on committees charged with using the material for judgment and decision making. This problem may be addressed by using an agreed-on organizing structure, including goals, preparation, appropriate methods, significant results, and a reflective critique (Glassick, Huber, and Maeroff, 1997).

The CEQ. The CEQ has been developed in Australia to gather feedback from recent graduates about their experience of their program in terms of five areas: (1) the quality of teaching, (2) clarity of goals, (3) workload, (4) assessment methods, and (5) development of generic skills (Johnson, 1999; Ramsden, 1991). The development of the CEQ has been a cumulative process based on the research by Ramsden and Entwistle (1981) in the United Kingdom on factors that promote deeper learning; the instrument has gone through several iterations and developments (Johnson, 1999; Wilson, Lizzio, and Ramsden, 1997).

The instrument seeks a response in relation to a whole program of study, for example, in engineering, history, or the performing arts. It therefore differs in level from conventional student evaluation that typically looks at individual instructors. In Australia, the CEQ was refined after a national trial of a broad range of indicators (Linke, 1991), and it provides systematic data about teaching, collected at the national level. The measure has been shown to be a stable, reliable, and meaningful source of evidence about the student experience of their educational programs (Hand and Trembath, 1998).

The instrument consists of twenty-four items that survey the five areas listed earlier, in addition to one global item measuring overall satisfaction with the student's program of study. Four examples of the twenty-five items used in the instrument are as follows:

- *Good teaching scale:* "The teaching staff of this course [program] motivated me to do my best work."
- *Appropriate workload scale:* "The workload was too heavy."

- *Generic skills:* "The course [program] developed my problem-solving skills."

CEQ data are now gathered each year from Australian graduates and used largely for internal diagnostic purposes by institutions and organizational units such as faculties or departments. Results from the instrument have also found their way into popular guides to universities that are used by prospective students to assist in their decision making about program choices.

As a performance indicator, the CEQ has been useful. First, having been used over a number of years, it is yielding data showing that in four of the five scales and the index of overall satisfaction, a positive national trend in improved teaching quality can be identified for the period from 1995 to 1998. This suggests that institutions are improving teaching quality and services to students (Johnson, 1999). Second, the CEQ is proving useful for making comparisons within fields of study over time and across institutions. Nevertheless, the significance of scores derived from the CEQ should always be interpreted in the context of specific institutional and program goals and circumstances (Hand and Trembath, 1998).

Internal Auditing. The application of financial auditing concepts to higher education institutions, including institutional teaching functions, is being tested in several countries (Holmes and Brown, 2000). Using the "six P's" of financial auditing, this approach is mainly prompted by external accountability demands for the *Purposes* of accountability and enhancement but also to generate information. Key *Participants* in the audit process are the auditors and those who are audited. It seems significant that students appear to have a minimal role in auditing. Diverse *Procedures* are used, ranging from auditors devising a methodology against the client's objectives to internally controlled, iterative procedures. In higher education there appears to be a degree of confusion about the appropriate audience for the *Product,* unlike financial audit reporting where there is a clearly defined audience, such as tax officials. Finally, the outcomes of an audit are meant to contribute to the development of *Policy.*

Hicks (2000) has described one example of the way the concept of audit has been applied at the University of Western Australia, where the Ensuring Teaching Quality—Best Practice Pathways (ETQ) is deployed as a self-audit approach. Hicks explicitly recognizes the contextual shift from teacher evaluation to a departmental focus for ensuring teaching quality. The ETQ is a four-page portfolio. It contains open-ended prompts for information about the promotion of learning and teaching in the department, course design, course delivery, assessment of learning, and the management of teaching. ETQ is described as an effective tool, both for accountability and for disseminating information about teaching practice.

Benchmarking. Benchmarking is a quality improvement technique that seeks to identify an organization that is doing something well, studying how it does this, and then applying the outcomes of the study to improving processes and outcomes in the home institution. It provides an external standard to help in the process of identifying where improvements might be made (Alstete, 1996; Jackson and Lund, 2000).

Benchmarking is analogous to the learning process and can be considered a method for learning how to improve. Therefore, benchmarking has the potential to fit comfortably in the higher education context, particularly as it relies on a methodology that requires hard data. It requires identifying the activities to be studied, specifying how the activity will be measured, deciding which other institutions to measure against, collecting the appropriate data, analyzing the data, identifying performance gaps, and developing recommendations. Jackson (2000) argues that benchmarking is no stranger to higher education. Principles of benchmarking, he suggests, are already embedded in practices such as the external examining of doctoral students and course accreditation carried out by professional bodies.

An examination of the literature suggests that, on the whole, benchmarking has been applied mainly to administrative procedures in higher education and in those areas of teaching activity that have strong, external, quality-oriented focus such as continuing education and business education (Alstete, 1996). Nevertheless, there have been attempts to use the methodology for learning and teaching. One example is the benchmarking system developed through extensive consultation with senior executives in Australian higher education institutions (McKinnon, Walker, and Davis, 2000).

Their manual contains sixty-seven benchmarks, grouped in categories including governance, impact, finance, learning and teaching, student support, research, and internationalization. Ten learning and teaching benchmark indicators are described: learning and teaching plans, course establishment processes, scholarly teaching, teaching environment, academic review processes, fitness of courses, retention, equity, student satisfaction, and employability. As a guide for implementation, each benchmark contains information about its rationale, sources of data, examples of good practice, and descriptive profiles for level of performance. So far, there are no published accounts of the outcomes of the approaches recommended in this manual.

Further approaches to benchmarking in the domain of teaching are described in the book by Jackson and Lund (2000). The following list is indicative of the comprehensive way in which benchmarking is being applied in the United Kingdom: key skills, the outcomes of learning, the student experience, departmental systems for managing standards, the learning environment, and educational processes.

Responsibility for Evaluation

In higher education, we have been reasonably successful in developing ways of collecting evidence about teaching, especially at the level of the individual teacher or course. But our understanding of how that evidence is used and by whom in order to make judgments and decisions is relatively poor (Mullins and Cannon, 1992). In fact, if we look at the way evaluative data are used, the situation is even gloomier: indeed, there seems to be good evidence that much of the information generated through surveys and the like is not actually used at all (Johnson, 1999).

It is in this domain of information use and decision making that I suspect we would find many of Scriven's shoddy practices. But it must be acknowledged that recent theoretical and policy work is confronting this issue (Centra, 2000; Glassick, Huber, and Maeroff, 1997). One thing that is changing is the much greater involvement in evaluation by different stakeholders. For example, students increasingly have access to the results of the ratings they provide. Faculty participate as colleagues and peers as well as evaluators on formal tenure and promotions committees. Expert evaluators (many of them faculty colleagues) take up responsibilities on external bodies as auditors, reviewers, and the like. This broadening of involvement ensures that diverse contexts are addressed in evaluating teaching and learning.

Conclusions

It is clear from this review of developments that the focus of evaluation is broadening. The focus is moving from the individual teacher toward the evaluation of teaching in its wider context. This is all to the good, because we now have a better understanding that a focus on decontextualized individuals is not a productive way to approach evaluation and change management process in higher education. A more educationally sound way is to create a context where evaluation is aligned (Biggs, 1999, 2001) and integrated across different levels.

We can see examples from the foregoing discussion of where alignment is emerging. Well-prepared portfolios, for example, demand that the alignment of objectives, methods, and outcomes be demonstrated and documented. The framework of standards for the evaluation of scholarship proposed by Glassick, Huber, and Maeroff (1997) is the most refined development of this idea to date. In an aligned system, the participants are "trapped" into engaging in appropriate practices—there can be no escape (Biggs, 2001).

In a contextually integrated system, evaluative processes are not only aligned but they are linked together vertically and horizontally. Vertically integrated evaluation happens when information from one level of evaluation (say, the evaluation of student learning) is used appropriately and ethically at another level, for example, by a teacher in a portfolio submitted in a tenure application or by a course review team. Some approaches to quality assurance now in use foster vertical integration by looking at the way evaluation is carried out and the way information is used rather than the actual data. Horizontal integration occurs when the information derived from an evaluation is actually used in a planned, strategic way. Most student evaluation data are not horizontally integrated.

If the principles and practices of evaluation could be aligned and integrated with the educational purposes of universities, then developments in the field may be characterized more by educational strategies than by strategies derived from economics, management, and business so much in evidence today.

Finally, I return to Scriven and offer an answer to his criticisms based on over two decades of development in the field of evaluation. Teacher evaluation is improving. The application of some practices may still be shoddy, but the principles are becoming clearer in the light of continuing research and development and a recognition of the importance of the context in which teaching and its evaluation is carried out. Recent work has suggested more ways to clarify the issues and to make the procedures more equitable and reasonably valid, but it remains difficult to point to a single exemplary system in which the practices come near to matching our knowledge. More attention needs to be focused on aligning and integrating evaluation, based on educational principles and on research-based decision making. The pressure to reform continues from outside as well as from inside the universities. But progress is being made. This chapter has sketched some ways that are beginning to improve our understanding of the complexity of the contexts in which to cast our evaluative efforts.

References

Alstete, J. W. *Benchmarking in Higher Education*. ASHE-ERIC Higher Education Report no 5. Washington, D.C.: The George Washington University Graduate School of Education and Human Development, 1996.

Barr, R. B., and Tagg, J. "From Teaching to Learning: A New Paradigm for Undergraduate Education." *Change*, 27(6), 13–25, 1995.

Biggs, J. "Enhancing Teaching through Constructive Alignment." *Higher Education*, 1996, 32, 347–364.

Biggs, J. *Teaching for Quality Learning*. Buckingham, England: Open University Press, 1999.

Biggs, J. "The Reflective Institution: Assuring and Enhancing the Quality of Teaching and Learning." *Higher Education*, 2001, 41, 221–238.

Cave, M., Hanney, S., Kogan, M., and Trevett, G. *The Use of Performance Indicators in Higher Education*. (3rd ed.) London: Jessica Kingsley, 1997.

Centra, J. A. "Evaluating the Teaching Portfolio: A Role for Colleagues." In K. E. Ryan (ed.), *Evaluating Teaching in Higher Education: A Vision for the Future*. New Directions for Teaching and Learning, no. 83. San Francisco: Jossey-Bass, 2000.

Dobson, I. "Appendix 1: Benchmarks in International League Tables." In K. R. McKinnon, S. H. Walker, and D. Davis (eds.), *Benchmarking: A Manual for Australian Universities*. Canberra: Department of Education, Training and Youth Affairs, 2000.

Edgerton, R., Hutchings, P., and Quinlan, K. *The Teaching Portfolio: Capturing the Scholarship of Teaching*. American Association for Higher Education, Washington, D.C., 1991.

Gaither, G. H., Nedwek, B. P., and Neal, J. E. *Measuring Up: The Promises and Pitfalls of Performance in Higher Education* ASHE-ERIC Higher Education Report no. 5.

Washington, D.C., Graduate School of Education and Human Development, The George Washington University, 1994.

Glassick, C. E., Huber, M. T., and Maeroff, G. I. *Scholarship Assessed: Evaluation of the Professoriate.* San Francisco: Jossey-Bass, 1997.

Hand, T., and Trembath, K. *Enhancing and Customising the Analysis of the Course Experience Questionnaire.* Canberra: Department of Employment, Training and Youth Affairs, 1998.

Hicks, O. "Ensuring Teaching Quality (ETQ)—Best Practice Pathways: A Focus on Departmental Practices for Good Teaching and Learning." In A Holmes and S. Brown (eds.), *Internal Audit in Higher Education.* London: Kogan Page, 2000.

Holmes, A., and Brown, S. (eds.). *Internal Audit in Higher Education.* London· Kogan Page, 2000.

Jackson, N. "Benchmarking Educational Processes and Outcomes." In N. Jackson and Lund, H. (eds.), *Benchmarking in Higher Education.* Buckingham, England: SRHE and Open University Press, 2000.

Jackson, N., and Lund, H. (eds.). *Benchmarking in Higher Education.* Buckingham, England: SRHE and Open University Press, 2000.

Johnson, T. *Course Experience Questionnaire, 1998.* Parkville, Victoria: Graduate Careers Council of Australia, 1999.

Johnson T. D., and Ryan K. E. "A Comprehensive Approach to the Evaluation of College Teaching." In K. E. Ryan (ed.), *Evaluating Teaching in Higher Education: A Vision for the Future.* New Directions for Teaching and Learning, no. 83. San Francisco: Jossey-Bass, 2000.

Kember, D. "A Reconceptualisation of the Research into University Academics' Conceptions of Teaching." *Learning and Instruction,* 1997, 7(3), 225–275.

Linke, R. D. *Performance Indicators in Higher Education: Report of a Trial Study Commissioned by the Commonwealth Department of Employment, Education and Training.* Canberra: Australian Government Publishing Service, 1991.

McKinnon, K. R., Walker, S. H., and Davis, D. *Benchmarking; A Manual for Australian Universities.* Canberra: Department of Education, Training and Youth Affairs, 2000.

Mullins, G. P., and Cannon, R. A. "A Teaching Portfolio for Departments." *Research and Development in Higher Education,* 1991, 13, 378–383.

Mullins, G. P., and Cannon, R. A. *Judging the Quality of Teaching.* Canberra: Australian Government Publishing Service, 1992.

Norris, D. M., and Malloch, T. R. *Unleashing the Power of Perpetual Learning.* Ann Arbor, Mich.: The Society for College and University Planning, 1997.

Pratt, D. D. "Reconceptualizing the Evaluation of Teaching in Higher Education." *Higher Education,* 1997, 34, 23–44.

Ramsden, P. "A Performance Indicator of Teaching Quality in Higher Education: The Course Experience Questionnaire." *Studies in Higher Education,* 1991, 16(2), 129–150.

Ramsden, P., and Entwistle, N. J. "Effects of Academic Departments on Students' Approaches to Studying." *British Journal of Educational Psychology,* 1981, 51, 368–383.

Scriven, M. "Summative Teacher Evaluation." In J. Millman, *Handbook of Teacher Evaluation.* Beverly Hills, Calif.: Sage, 1981.

Scriven M. *Evaluation Thesaurus.* (4th ed.) Beverly Hills, Calif.: Sage, 1991.

Shore, B., and Associates. *The Teaching Dossier: Guide to its Preparation and Use.* Ottawa: Canadian Association of University Teachers, 1986.

Wilson, K., Lizzio, A., and Ramsden, P. "The Development, Validation and Application of the Course Experience Questionnaire." *Studies in Higher Education,* 22(1), 1997, 33–53.

ROBERT CANNON *is associate professor and director of the Advisory Centre for University Education at Adelaide University, South Australia.*

INDEX

SINGLE ISSUE SALE

For a limited time save 10% on single issues! Save an additional 10% when you purchase three or more single issues. Each issue is normally 27^{00}.

Please see the next page for a complete listing of available back issues.

Mail or fax this completed form to: Jossey-Bass, A Wiley Company
989 Market Street • Fifth Floor • San Francisco CA 94103-1741

CALL OR FAX
Phone 888-378-2537 or 415-433-1740 *or Fax* 800-605-2665 or 415-433-4611 *(attn customer service)*
BE SURE TO USE PROMOTION CODE ND2 TO GUARANTEE YOUR DISCOUNT!
Please send me the following issues at 24^{30} each.

(Important: please include series initials and issue number, such as TL87)

1. TL _____

_____

_____

$ _____ Total for single issues (24^{30} each)

_____ Less 10% if ordering 3 or more issues

_____ SHIPPING CHARGES: SURFACE   Domestic   Canadian

	Domestic	Canadian
First Item	$5.00	$6.50
Each Add'l Item	$3.00	$3.00

For next-day and second-day delivery rates, call the number listed above.

$ _____ Total (Add appropriate sales tax for your state. Canadian residents add GST)

❑ Payment enclosed (U.S. check or money order only)

❑ VISA, MC, AmEx Discover Card # _____ Exp. date _____

Signature _____

Day phone _____

❑ Bill me (U.S. institutional orders only. Purchase order required)
Purchase order # _____
   Federal Tax ID. 135593032   GST 89102 8052

Name _____

Address _____

_____

Phone _____ E-mail _____

For more information about Jossey-Bass, visit our website at: www.josseybass.com

OFFER EXPIRES FEBRUARY 28, 2002.   **PROMOTION CODE = ND2**

Save Now on the Best of ABOUT CAMPUS Series Sets
Enriching the Student Learning Experience

Dedicated to the idea that student learning is the responsibility of all educators on campus, **About Campus** illuminates critical issues faced by both student affairs and academic affairs staff as they work on the shared goal that brought them to the same campus in the first place: to help students learn.

With each issue, **About Campus** combines the imagination and creativity found in the best magazines and the authority and thoughtfulness found in the best professional journals. Now we've taken the four most popular issues from three volume years and we've made them available as a set— at a tremendous savings over our $20.00 single issue price.

Best of About Campus – Volume 3

Facts and Myths About Assessment in Student Affairs – Why Learning Communities? Why Now? – The Stressed Student: How Can We Help? – Being All That We Can Be
ISBN 0–7879–6128–0 $12.00

Best of About Campus – Volume 4

Increasing Expectations for Student Effort – The Matthew Shepard Tragedy: Crisis and Beyond – Civic and Moral Learning – Faculty-Student Affairs Collaboration on Assessment.
ISBN 0–7879–6129–9 $12.00

Best of About Campus – Volume 5

The Diversity Within – What Can We Do About Student Cheating – Bonfire: Tragedy and Tradition – Hogwarts: The Learning Community.
ISBN 0–7879–6130–2 $12.00

To order by phone: call 1–800–956–7739 or 415–433–1740
Visit our website at www.josseybass.com

Use promotion code **ND2** to guarantee your savings.
Shipping and applicable taxes will be added.

ABOUT CAMPUS

Sponsored by the *American College Personnel Association*
Published by Jossey-Bass, A Wiley Company

Patricia M. King, Executive Editor
Jon C. Dalton, Senior Editor

Published bimonthly. Individual subscriptions $53.00. Institutional subscriptions $95.00.

Jossey-Bass, A Wiley Company • 989 Market St., Fifth Floor • San Francisco, CA 94103–1741

TL87 **Techniques and Strategies for Interpreting Student Evaluations**
Karron G. Lewis
Focuses on all phases of the student rating process—from data gathering
methods to presentation of results. Topics include methods of encouraging
meaningful evaluations, midsemester feedback, uses of quality teams and
focus groups, and creating questions that target individual faculty needs and
interest.
ISBN· 0-7879-5789-5

TL86 **Scholarship Revisited: Perspectives on the Scholarship of Teaching**
Carolin Kreber
Presents the outcomes of a Delphi Study conducted by an international
panel of academics working in faculty evaluation scholarship and
postsecondary teaching and learning. Identifies the important components of
scholarship of teaching, defines its characteristics and outcomes, and
explores its most pressing issues.
ISBN: 0-7879-5447-0

TL85 **Beyond Teaching to Mentoring**
Alice G. Reinarz, Eric R. White
Offers guidelines to optimizing student learning through classroom activities
as well as peer, faculty, and professional mentoring. Addresses mentoring
techniques in technical training, undergraduate business, science, and liberal
arts studies, health professions, international study, and interdisciplinary
work.
ISBN: 0-7879-5617-1

TL84 **Principles of Effective Teaching in the Online Classroom**
Renée E. Weiss, Dave S. Knowlton, Bruce W. Speck
Discusses structuring the online course, using resources from the World
Wide Web, and using other electronic tools and technology to enhance
classroom efficiency. Addresses challenges unique to the online classroom
community, including successful communication strategies, performance
evaluation, academic integrity, and accessibility for disabled students.
ISBN: 0-7879-5615-5

TL83 **Evaluating Teaching in Higher Education: A Vision for the Future**
Katherine E. Ryan
Analyzes the strengths and weaknesses of current approaches to evaluating
teaching and recommends practical strategies for improving current
evaluation methods and developing new ones. Provides an overview of new
techniques such as peer evaluations, portfolios, and student ratings of
instructors and technologies.
ISBN: 0-7879-5448-9

TL82 **Teaching to Promote Intellectual and Personal Maturity: Incorporating
Students' Worldviews and Identities into the Learning Process**
Marcia B. Baxter Magolda

Explores cognitive and emotional dimensions that influence how individuals learn and describes teaching practices for building on these to help students develop intellectually and personally. Examines how students' unique understanding of their individual experience, themselves, and the ways knowledge is constructed can mediate learning.
ISBN: 0-7879-5446-2

TL81   **Strategies for Energizing Large Classes: From Small Groups to Learning Communities**
Jean MacGregor, James L. Cooper, Karl A. Smith, Pamela Robinson
Describes a comprehensive range of ideas and techniques from informal "turn-to-your-neighbor" discussions that punctuate a lecture to more complex small-group activities as well as ambitious curricular reform through learning-community structures.
ISBN. 0-7879-5337-7

TL80   **Teaching and Learning on the Edge of the Millennium: Building on What We Have Learned**
Marilla D. Svinicki
Reviews the past and current research on teaching, learning, and motivation. Chapters revisit the best-selling *NDTL* issues, exploring the latest developments in group-based learning, effective communication, teaching for critical thinking, the seven principles for good practice in undergraduate education, teaching for diversity, and teaching in the information age.
ISBN: 0-7879-4874-8

TL79   **Using Consultants to Improve Teaching**
Christopher Knapper, Sergio Piccinin
Provides advice on how to use consultation to improve teaching, giving detailed descriptions of a variety of effective approaches, including classroom observation, student focus groups, small group instructional diagnosis, faculty learning communities, and action learning.
ISBN: 0-7879-4876-4

TL78   **Motivation from Within: Approaches for Encouraging Faculty and Students to Excel**
Michael Theall
Examines how students' cultural backgrounds and beliefs about knowledge affect their motivation to learn and applies the latest motivational theory to the instructional process and the university community.
ISBN: 0-78794875-6

TL77   **Promoting Civility: A Teaching Challenge**
Steven M. Richardson
Offers strategies for promoting civil discourse and resolving conflict when it arises—both in the classroom and in the campus community at-large. Recommends effective responses to disruptive classroom behavior and techniques for encouraging open, respectful discussion of sensitive topics.
ISBN: 0-7879-4277-4

TL76   **The Impact of Technology on Faculty Development, Life, and Work**
Kay Herr Gillespie
Describes ways to enhance faculty members' technological literacy, suggests an approach to instructional design that incorporates the possibilities of

today's technologies, and examines how the on-line community offers an expansion of professional relationships and activities.
ISBN: 0-7879-4280-4

TL75 **Classroom Assessment and Research: An Update on Uses, Approaches, and Research Findings**
Thomas Angelo
Illustrates how classroom assessment techniques (CATs) enhance both student learning and the scholarship of teaching. Demonstrates how CATs can promote good teamwork in students, help institutions answer the call for program accountability, and guide new teachers in developing their teaching philosophies.
ISBN: 0-7879-9885-0

TL74 **Changing the Way We Grade Student Performance: Classroom Assessment and the New Learning Paradigm**
Rebecca S. Anderson, Bruce W. Speck
Offers alternative approaches to assessing student performance that are rooted in the belief that students should be active rather than passive learners. Explains how to use each assessment measure presented, including developing criteria, integrating peer and self-assessment, and assigning grades.
ISBN: 0-7879-4278-2

TL73 **Academic Service Learning: A Pedagogy of Action and Reflection**
Robert A. Rhoads, Jeffrey P.F. Howard
Presents an academic conception of service learning, described as "a pedagogical model that intentionally integrates academic learning and relevant community service." Describes successful programs and discusses issues that faculty and administrators must consider as they incorporate service learning into courses and curricula.
ISBN: 0-7879-4276-6

TL72 **Universal Challenges in Faculty Work: Fresh Perspectives from Around the World**
Patricia Cranton
Educators from around the world describe issues they face in their teaching practice. National differences are put into the context of universal themes including responding to demands for social development and reacting to influences by government policies and financial constraints.
ISBN: 0-7879-3961-7

TL71 **Teaching and Learning at a Distance: What It Takes to Effectively Design, Deliver, and Evaluate Programs**
Thomas E. Cyrs
Offers insights from experienced practitioners into what is needed to make teaching and learning at a distance successful for everyone involved.
ISBN: 0-7879-9884-2

TL70 **Approaches to Teaching Non-Native English Speakers Across the Curriculum**
David L. Sigsbee, Bruce W. Speck, Bruce Maylath
Provides strategies that help students who are non-native users of English improve their writing and speaking skills in content-area courses. Considers

the points of view of the students themselves and discusses their differing levels of intent about becoming proficient in English writing and speaking.
ISBN: 0-7879-9860-5

TL69   **Writing to Learn: Strategies for Assigning and Responding to Writing Across the Disciplines**
Mary Deane Sorcinelli, Peter Elbow
Presents strategies and philosophies about the way writing is learned, both in the context of a discipline and as an independent skill. Focusing primarily on the best ways to give feedback about written work, the authors describe a host of alternatives that have a solid foundation in research.
ISBN: 0-7879-9859-1

TL68   **Bringing Problem-Based Learning to Higher Education: Theory and Practice**
LuAnn Wilkerson, Wim H. Gijselaers
Describes the basics of problem-based learning along with the variables that affect its success. Provides examples of its application in a wide range of disciplines, including medicine, business, education, engineering, mathematics, and the sciences.
ISBN: 0-7879-9934-2

TL67   **Using Active Learning in College Classes: A Range of Options for Faculty**
Tracey E. Sutherland, Charles C. Bonwell
Examines the use of active learning in higher education and describes the concept of the active learning continuum, tying various practical examples of active learning to that concept.
ISBN: 0-7879-9933-4

TL66   **Ethical Dimensions of College and University Teaching: Understanding and Honoring the Special Relationship Between Teachers and Students**
Linc Fisch
Illustrates that responsibility to students is directly related to understanding of one's ethical self, and the first step in establishing that ethical identity is self-reflection. Details the transformation of structures and attitudes that ethical teaching fosters.
ISBN: 0-7879-9910-5

TL65   **Honoring Exemplary Teaching**
Marilla D. Svinicki, Robert J. Menges
Describes programs for faculty recognition in a variety of settings and with varying purposes. Reviews research relevant to selection criteria and offers guidelines for planning and implementing effective programs.
ISBN· 0-7879-9979-2

TL64   **Disciplinary Differences in Teaching and Learning: Implications for Practice**
Nira Hativa, Michele Marincovich
Discusses causes and consequences of disciplinary differences in the patterns of teaching and learning; in the instructional strategies to increase teaching effectiveness; in the culture and environment in which teaching takes place; and in faculty and students' attitudes, goals, beliefs, values, philosophies, and orientations toward instruction.
ISBN: 0-7879-9909-1

Lightning Source UK Ltd.
Milton Keynes UK
22 July 2010

9 780787 957902